ROBOTS HOW INFLUENCE MARKETING DEVELOPMENT

JOHN LOK

Copyright © John Lok
All Rights Reserved.

This book has been published with all efforts taken to make the material error-free after the consent of the author. However, the author and the publisher do not assume and hereby disclaim any liability to any party for any loss, damage, or disruption caused by errors or omissions, whether such errors or omissions result from negligence, accident, or any other cause.

While every effort has been made to avoid any mistake or omission, this publication is being sold on the condition and understanding that neither the author nor the publishers or printers would be liable in any manner to any person by reason of any mistake or omission in this publication or for any action taken or omitted to be taken or advice rendered or accepted on the basis of this work. For any defect in printing or binding the publishers will be liable only to replace the defective copy by another copy of this work then available.

Contents

Preface

Prepare

How AI technology influence productivities and service performance ? How AI can predict consumer behaviors. This book aims to explain why and how future artificial intelligent technology (big data gathering method) can be applied to assit businesses to predict why and when and how consumer behavior changes. I shall explain why traditional psychological and statistic and marketing methods are applied to predict consumer behaviors, human's judgement and analytical effort will be worse to compare AI machine's judgement and analytical effort. Also, I shall indicate different business organizations why they apply AI big data gathering method to help them to design any questionnaires (surveys) questions which will be more valid and useful to conclude human's questionnaires (surveys) design questions method.

This book has these two research questions need to be answered. Can apply (AI) learning machine predict consumer behaviors? Can (AI) learning machine replace human marketing research method, e.g. survey or human psychological and micro and macro economic methods to predict consumer behaviors more accurate?

Nowadays, many businessmen or marketing research professional hope to apply different methods to predict consumer behaviors in order to know what will be future market activities and market changes to help them to choose to implement what kinds of marketing strategies more accurately. The methods include economic environmental change prediction method, consumer individual psychological change prediction method, micro or macro behavioral economic environmental change prediction method, marketing environmental change prediction method etc. different kinds of methods which can be applied to predict how consumer behavioral changes to influence whose behavioral consumption to the manufacturer products sale within one to two years short term or three to five years middle term, even above five years long term business plans.

Hence, if the product manufacturers can apply the most suitable consumer behavioral prediction method to predict how consumers' choice will be changed to influence their products sale easily. It will have more beneficial intangible and tangible advantages to achieve the their product easier sale aim to ensure their businesses' future market share to be increased more easier to their countries' choice target sale markets. Otherwise, if they applied the inaccurate consumer behavioral prediction methods to predict how their consumers' behavioral changes wrongly. Then, it will influence their market shares to be same level, even it will decrease their market shares, when their consumer behavioral prediction inaccurately.

In my this book first part, I concentrate on indicate whether any artificial intelligence (AI) tools will be one kind of good consumer behavioral prediction method to be choose to apply to predict consumer behaviors. I shall indicate some examples, cases to give reasonable evidences to analyze whether (AI) tools will be one kind suitable tool to be applied to predict when and how consumer behavioral changes. If (AI) can be one kind tool to attempt to be applied to predict when and how consumer behavioral changes. Will it replace other kinds of methods to predict consumer behaviors? Does it have weaknesses to be applied to predict consumer behaviors, instead of strengths? Can it be applied to predict consumer behaviors depending on any situations of only some situation? Finally, I believe that any readers can find answers to answer above these questions in this book.

In my this book second part, I shall explain why and how human can possible apply (AI) tool to predict consumer individual emotion. I shall indicate case studies to explain how consumer individual better or worse emotion how to influence whose consumption behavior in different situation. Finally, I shall indicate evidences to conclude how and why (AI) tool that can be used to predict consumer individual emotion and it will have direct relationship to influence consumption behavior, as well as how (AI) tool can assist businessmen to judge whether what reasons case the customer does not choose to buy its product, it is possible because the product high price factor, poor product quality or poor staff service performance or attitude etc. different factors to influence the consumer decides to choose to buy the other product consequently, when the (AI) tool can confirm consumer has good or bad emotion to judge what factors are the causes his decision making at the moment.

Readers can understand why and how (AI) tool can be attempt to be applied to predict customer emotion and it can influence positive or negative consumption behavior to the product clearly in this part.

This book third part has these two research questions need to be answered? Can apply (AI) learning machine as well as micro and macro economic methods predict consumer behavioral changing?Can (AI) learning machine replace human marketing research method, e.g. survey or human psychological and micro and macro economic methods to predict consumer behaviors more accurate?

The part indicates whether micro and macro economic methods can be attempted to apply to predict when, how and why consumer behavioral changing for every kind of different business. The second part indicates whether artificial intelligence can be attempted to apply to predict when, how and why consumer behavioral changing for every kind of different business.

Nowadays, many businessmen or marketing research professional hope to apply different methods to predict consumer behaviors in order to know what will be future market activities and market changes to help them to choose to implement what kinds of marketing strategies more accurately.

The methods include economic environmental change prediction method, consumer individual psychological change prediction method, micro or macro behavioral economic environmental change prediction method, marketing environmental change prediction method etc. different kinds of methods which can be applied to predict how consumer behavioral changes to influence whose behavioral consumption to the manufacturer products sale within one to two years short term or three to five years middle term, even above five years long term business plans.

Hence, if the product manufacturers can apply the most suitable consumer behavioral prediction method to predict how consumers' choice will be changed to influence their products sale easily. It will have more beneficial intangible and tangible advantages to achieve the their product easier sale aim to ensure their businesses' future market share to be increased more easier to their countries' choice target sale markets. Otherwise, if they applied the inaccurate consumer behavioral prediction methods to predict how their consumers' behavioral changes wrongly. Then, it will influence their market shares to be same level, even it will decrease their market shares, when their consumer behavioral prediction inaccurately.

Whether can businessmen apply micro and macro-economic methods to assist them to analyze how marketing will change, what marketing trend will develop next month or next half year, even more than one year marketing development trend in possible?

In my this book final part, I shall considerate on businessmen and customers both beneficial view point to explain how to apply behavioral economic concept to predict how their specific industries marketing development trend or consumer behavioral changing trend in these micro economic (individual consumer psychological shopping change trend) and macro-economic (global every specific industry marketing changing trend) environment.

This third part researches this two questions: Has it relationship between macro and micro economic environment change factors to influence marketing development change trend? Can businessmen apply macro and micro economic methods to predict future marketing development change trend in their specific industries?

I shall indicate some specific cases industry to attempt to explain whether it has really relationship between macro and micro economic environment change factors to influence marketing development change trend as well as whether businessmen can apply micro and macro-economic methods to predict future marketing development change trend in these specific industries.

In my this part, I concentrate on indicate whether any artificial intelligence (AI) tools will be one kind of good consumer behavioral prediction method to be choose to apply to predict consumer behaviors. I shall indicate some examples, cases to give reasonable evidences to analyze whether (AI) tools will be one kind suitable tool to be applied to predict when and how consumer behavioral changes. If (AI) can be one kind tool to attempt to be applied to predict when and how consumer behavioral changes. Will it replace other kinds of methods to predict consumer behaviors? Does it have weaknesses to be applied to predict consumer behaviors, instead of strengths? Can it be applied to predict consumer behaviors depending on any situations of only some situation? Finally, I believe that any readers can find answers to answer above these questions in this book.

In my analysis, I conclude marketing development or marketing change trend will be influenced by consumer behavioral change model or attitude factor. Finally, I hope my readers can give opinions to make judgement to evaluate my opinions whether is right or wrong in this research topic.

In part four, I shall indicate sample case study to judge whether it is possible to apply (AI) tool to attempt to help businesses to predict consumer behaviors in different business environment.

Prologue

CHAPTER ONE

(AI) prediction consumer behavior tool

1.1 How can artificial intelligent tools predict consumer behavior in vehicle market

What is (AI) consumer behavioral prediction tool? How any why will (AI) tool assist manufactures to attempt to predict consumer behavior before and after consumption occurrence? First, I shall indicate how to apply (AI) tool to predict vehicle product consumer behavior case example. Nowadays, many vehicle manufacturers hope their vehicles can attract to vehicle buyers to choose to buy their vehicles. However, there are many different brands of vehicles to provide to them to choose, so the vehicle market competition is very serious.

How to judge their different kinds of vehicle price which is reasonable acceptance to attract vehicle buyers to choose to buy the brand of vehicle manufacturers' any kinds of vehicles, e.g. fast speed sport style vehicles, comfortable and slow speed common cars, for four passengers common small size or more than four passengers common large car size? How to evaluate the vehicle prices issue is important factor to influence vehicle buyers' choices. Either if the brand of vehicle price is too high to compare brands, it will influence many vehicle buyers choose to buy other brands' vehicles or if the brand of vehicle price is too low, it will influence vehicle buyers feel this brand's vehicle's quality is worse to compare to other vehicle brands' similar vehicle products.

Thus, if the brand of vehicle manufacturers can predict how to design vehicles which can attract many vehicle buyers to choose to buy whose any vehicle products. What are future vehicle buyers' favorable vehicle styles? Then, the vehicle manufacturer can concentrate on manufacturing the kind style of vehicle products to sell already. It will reduce its vehicle manufacturing investment risk.

How to apply (AI) tools to predict vehicle buyers' behavioral consumption model? Whether artificial intelligent tools can predict automotive buyers' behavioral consumption model and predict future trend. In fact, automotive brands and dealerships are facing an increasingly competition when attempting to manually gathering the vast quantities of data required to create customer focused programs that increase retention, ultimately new sales and service automotive business. Building a based on that client's intrinsic needs and interests to any kinds of automotive vehicles at any given time. This is especially true in the automotive industry where the time span between purchases is measured in years. Because vehicle buyers would not like often to change their old vehicle to another new one. So, their decisions to buying another new vehicle, the time is usually after one year, even longer time. Hence, it seems any vehicles won't be frequent consumption products to the owned at least one vehicle family consumers (vehicle buyers).

Hence, how to predict vehicle consumers' taste or preferable which styles of vehicle choices issues is very important. If the vehicle manufacturers can not manufacture any attractive vehicles to sell easily in this year. Then, it will lose time, money in this year because it won't know when the owned least one vehicle users or non-owned any vehicle users who will decide to buy one new vehicle or change another new vehicle ensure. The different brand vehicle dealers will possible wait more than one year to attract them to buy their vehicles if their styles are not attractive to compare other brands of vehicle competitors.

However, artificial intelligence and machine learning can help any vehicle manufacturers to find solution to solve patterns in highly to solve patterns in highly complex data-sets that are beyond the capability of a human brain, and then building and automatically acting on the customer insights it generates.

Given the automotive customer need for individualized communications, this technology is positioned to become a critical component of any successful vehicle retailer's domestic or/and overseas vehicle markets. How can vehicle manufacturers and retailers use (AI) to enhance their vehicle marketing campaigns? How will (AI) affect their vehicle sale marketing strategy? What criteria would they use when selecting on (AI) solution?

Vehicle consumers today are able to quickly access different brands of vehicle information, research vehicle products and reviews, negotiate prices and compare one vehicle brand or retailer to another resulting of the brands of vehicle customers. At the same time, the rise of " big -data mining", wearable devices that track user's every move and preference and greater contextualization in advertising and social media has resulted in consumer expectations of individualized. Thus, it seems that (AI) tools can be used to gather " big-data" and then they can make human's mind to analyze how to design kinds of vehicles to satisfy vehicle buyers' needs.

As automotive vehicle marketers can apply (AI) tools to achieve messaging strategies to meet the needs of this new generation of informed vehicle consumers, using data from a variety of sources to move from a variety of sources to move from mass- messaging to more personalized messages aimed at particular vehicle buyer segments, e.g. fast speed sport vehicle buyer segment, slow speed comfortable small size or large size of buyer segment. However, when 90% of vehicle marketers believe having a single vehicle buyer view is important, only 6% have achieved it.

However, one of the main issues vehicle marketers facing is the lack of capacity to efficiently sift through and analyze the massive vehicle buyer amounts of data required to create vehicle buyer individualized vehicle customer experiences easily. This is especially difficult for automotive dealers, the long periods between purchase cycles, and the highly considered nature of the vehicle purchase means that each vehicle dealer needs to not only track a large number of potential vehicle customers for an extremely long period of time, but each of those vehicle customers will generate a huge amount of different kinds of vehicle behavioral consumption data as they research their next vehicle purchase. However, by choosing the right (AI) technological tools and programs , vehicle dealers can solve this big data gathering challenge into a major advantage.

For Forrester vehicle brand example, vehicle consumers have more power over the Forrester vehicle brand's reputation than ever before. Mayne, L. (2014) indicated that Forrester calls this new (AI) tools is the " age of the vehicle customer", a 20 year business cycle in which the most successful vehicle enterprises will reinvent themselves to systematically understand and serve increasingly powerful vehicle consumers. To win in this new age, Forrester declares companies must become vehicle customer obsessed and the only sustainable competitive advantage is knowledge and engagement with customers, such as (AI) gathering data knowledge.

Thus, the biggest challenge vehicle businesses currently face is not the collection of a large quantity of vehicle consumer data, but what to do with that data once they have it. Even at a large vehicle data research firm, the data sets are often too big for a single analyze, or even a team of analysts to sort through and draw conclusion from. However, enter artificial intelligence and machine learning , an efficient technology solution that can continuously find patterns in highly complex data sets that are way beyond the capacity of a human brain and then automatic drive action based on the customer insights is generated.

What is (AI) machine learning tool? Machine learning is a type of (AI) that learns from data and is not explicitly program. Think Amazon, face book. Machine learning serves up relevant content based on an individual vehicle purchase behavior and experiences. More simply, machine learning is a computer program that can learn relationships between data, subject those learnings to errors functions, and then learn from its errors. The program in effect, trains itself.

Lee, T. (2016) explained that "Thus, (AI) tools can learn deep a more advanced branch of machine learning inspired by how our brain's nervous function, has also been found to be especial effective in identifying patterns from data."

When this way sound is complicated from a vehicle dealer perspective, the implementation of a marketing program driven by artificial intelligence can take care of these tasks in an automatic vehicle fashion with little to no manual intervention required from the staff at time vehicle stores.

In practice at a vehicle dealership, the program will continue track vehicle customer behavior online, merging that data with any offline source (like CRM or DMS data) and then analyze this aggregated vehicle buyer data set to predict what vehicle customer may be shopping for and what information they might like to relevance from different kinds style of vehicle design photos.

1.1 Why can (AI) be applied to predict consumer behaviors?

Artificial intelligence refers to complex in vehicle market, machine learning that posses the same characteristics of human intelligence and that have all our sense, all our reason and think just like human do. Besides, machine learning is the practice of using algorithms to collect and examine data, learn from it, and then make a determination or prediction about something in the world.

The machine is " trained" using large amounts of data and algorithms that give it the ability to learn how to automatically perform a task with increasing accuracy. Otherwise, deep learning is primarily based on artificial neural networks inspired by our understanding of the biology of human's brains.

Deep learning breaks down tasks in ways that enables machines to assist us with increasingly complex tasks, driverless cars, better preventive healthcare and more accurate product recommendation (including vehicle recommendations). So, such as why (AI) technology can be applied to predict how vehicle consumer behavior changes to bring to judge whether vehicle consumer will like what kinds of vehicle styles next year. Then, vehicle manufacturers can gather overall vehicle consumer data to analyze and conclude the more accurate vehicle design direction for next year any new design vehicle manufacturing products.

Thus, (AI) machine learning can help vehicle manufacturers to solve how to design any new vehicle products challenge. A vehicle is both one of the most important and carefully considered purchases the majority of people will ever make in their lifetime. It is also a purchase that tends to be fundamentally tied to a person's identify and view of themselves. As the same time, vehicle consumers changing lifestyles result in changing vehicle needs, e.g. the young sport car enthusiast matures into the family driver.

Automotive dealers need to remember that vehicle customers and prospects are individual human beings with risk, complex and ever-changing lives factors, these factors will influence every vehicle consumer why who feels has vehicle purchase need, and how who choose to buy the first vehicle if who decided to buy the first vehicle.

The (AI) technological customer behavioral prediction tool seems to be the best vehicle salespeople in the world are those that know every one of their vehicle customers. Their likes and dislikes which style of vehicle design, preferences and changing tastes to vehicle choices. The capacity of the human brain, however, limits us from achieving this type of vehicle sales and frequent turnover at vehicle dealerships often results in the further loss of vehicle salespeople along with their vehicle customer relationships and knowledge. In this competitive vehicle environment, machine learning enables platforms to assist the vehicle sales team by tracking the vehicle consumer behaviors of each vehicle customer, learning and memorizing their preferences and predicting their future vehicle purchase needs.

Finally, I recommend that for a vehicle dealerships marketing platform to make their customer engagement efficient and fully-functional, I should be able to: applying (AI) tools to track every vehicle customer behavior across the web, connecting to a society of data sources, CRM, DMS, third-party, web vehicle brands, social email, click etc., aggregating and accurately cross-reference data from a variety of sources, leveraging this data to drive insights on a mass scale, as well as on an individualized basis, driving actions and automatically direct customer engagement via multiple channels based on where each customer is in their individual lifecycle.

1.2 How can (AI) provide businesses with better-informed decisions

I shall explain how (AI) technology can provide businesses with better-informed decisions to drive top-line growth, deliver meaningful experience for customers and smooth their path along the consumer journey. The widely understood definition of (AI) involves the ability of machines or computers to learn human thinking, reasoning and decision-making abilities.

A Narrative science study in 2015 year identified that (AI) was being used primarily in voice recognition, machine learning virtual assistants and decision support. This study also highlighted the many branches of (AI) and that techniques and their definition are used interchangeably. It is possible that (AI) can be used to gather big data , then to analyze to help businesses to predict consumer behaviors. For example, one of the most common techniques is machine learning, where algorithms are used to perform tasks by learning from historical data. Another growth branch of (AI) is natural language procession.

However, during 2017 year, search engines will begin to factor additional behavioral data into prediction of customer behavioral results, such as the user's history of searches and locations and previously captures conservations. Artificial intelligence will use this information to power predictive search results, e.g. predictive future consumer's choice behavioral processing for any kinds of businesses.

Predictive search will improve the quality of search results, and provide new insights into consumers' behavior and the moments which matter to them. Search will give recommendation into tailored how consumer individual choice in consumption process. Several of the largest online platforms already use machine learning to improve predictive consumer behavioral search results.

For example, Google's rank brain technology adds research by understanding the context in which the consumer has entered it. Over time, rank brain will learn further from user behaviors Amazon's DSSTNE (pronounced destiny) learns from shoppers' purchasing habits and consumption behavior to offer better product recommend actions, which Amazon can offer before a consumer has entered anything into the search bar. However, this technology is not independent of human input. For example, Google engineers will periodically retain the rank brain system to improve the models it uses. For another example, in 2016 year , Apple computer revamped its photos app to allow consumers to search for specific items in the phots, they want to find, not just dates and locations. Each photo that an intelligent phone or intelligent pad user takes goes through 11 billion computations, so that photos can understand exactly what is the photography.

It seems that in future, (AI) machine learning will allow search to evolve even further. Search engineers will deliver refined recommendations to their business users and use less human input to predict consumers' needs. For IBM computer example, it indicated 90% of the data that exists today has been created in the last two years. This huge explosion of data gives brands the opportunity to quickly spot and react to the latest trends, fashion and fads among its clients and potential clients. This will allow companies to better engage with younger consumers, who gain influence access to the latest trends, and use the brands. They associate with to help define who they are as individuals. Thus, brands have to identify and make use of them before consumers move on, but the vast quantity of data available makes. This a resource-intensive task. For next example, Lesara, a based online clothes store, uses this machine learning to inform its product decision often gathering information from internal and external sources. When its trends -spotting shoes. Lesara has a range of over 20 styles and sells hundreds of pairs a day. It focus on giving consumers, the very latest trends allow Lesara to develop on average of 50,000 new items each year. It compared to 11,000 old items each year. Thus, (AI) brain seems to human brain to own analytical ability to predict consumer behaviors.

For another example, Lesara is one online clothes store, uses machine learning decisions after gathering information from internal and external sources. One of its most popular products, shoes with LED started life when its trend spotting software flagged up a blogger wearing similar shoes. Now Lesara has a range of over 20 styles and sells hundreds of pairs a day. Its focus on giving consumers the very latest trends allows Lesara to develop an average of 50,000 new items each year, compared to 11,000 for its competitor Lara. it seems (AI) machine learning can help Lesara business to predict what kinds of shoes design or style that shoe consumers will prefer choose to buy in future shoe market trend. Thus, Lesara can predict shoe consumers' taste successfully and it can manufacture many attractive style of shoes. (AI) machine learning can gather global past shoe consumer's shoe shopping experiences, then analyzes to make conclusion to give lesara recommendation successfully. This will make the experience more enjoyable for shoe consumers and allow Lesara to advert whose different new style or design of shoes to deliver them move relevant messages by understanding the context of the experience.

However, (AI) machine learning will have this risk who manufacturers need to concern if they applied this technology to predict consumer behavior. It is on sample consumers' privacy issue, in order to avoid complaint chance occurrence. However, machine learning can tie this data together to identify which f the billions of devices are being used by individual consumers. This helps brands understand how consumer engagement and actions can be attributed to different messages in different contexts and at different time. So, machine learning can help brands to build confidence to promote their products by any advertisement channels. When, this new (AI) machine learning technology can conclude how to design their products to be the most attractive, due to it has more accurate to predict consumer behaviors to compare human themselves prediction judgement effort. It seems that (AI) machine judgement effort is more accurate to compare to human judgment effort.

For example, google is moving away from cookies and using logged in data to track and make to users. It plans to expand the scope of the brand lift tool from online video. Thus, consumers are responded will to shippable context, finding it persuasive and easy to navigate by (AI) machine learning decision. For example, fashion brands can aggregate their You tub videos and blogs into a mobile context marketing experience, such as brand centric context into a personal shopping activity gives the shopper an experience, who are likely to remember and tell their friends about any new style of products design promotion from these internet advertisement channels after (AI) machine learning tools' styles of product design recommendation.

What is (AI) deep learning techniques to forecast environment behavioral consumption

The (AI) deep-learning technology leads to performance enhancement and generalization of artificial intelligent technology. It influences the global leader in the field of information technology has declared its intention to utilize the deep-learning technology to solve environmental problems, such as climate change. So, it will help agriculture farming businesses can raise any plant food: vegetable, fruit, rice which grow up very easily if farmers can apply (AI) deep-learning technology to solve environment problems to influence their plant food grow. If the whole year seasonal change is very good and it is suitable for any plant food to grow in farming land easily, e.g. rain is enough and soil is enough for any plant food to grow in the farm lands. Then, fruit, rice, vegetable etc. agriculture businesses will have much beneficial attribution to global farmers.

The question is how to use deep-learning technologies in the environmental field to predict the status of pro-environmental consumption. We predicted the pro-environmental consumption index based on Google search query data, using a recurrent neural network (RNN model). To certify the accuracy of the index, we compared the prediction accuracy of the RNN model with that of the ordinary least square and artificial necessary network models. For example, the RNN model predicts the pro-environmental consumption index better than any other model. we expect the RNN model to perform still better in a big data environment because the deep-learning technologies would be increasingly as the volume of data grows. So, deep-learning technologies could be useful in environmental forecasting to prevent damage caused by climate change to influence any rice, vegetable, tomato, potato, fruit etc. different plant food grow in any countries' farming land easily.

For South Korea example, over 800 government agencies spent 2.2 trillion Korea won on eco-products in 2014 year. However, green products are rarely purchased outside these agencies. This phenomenon occurs because there is a gap between consumer attitudes and behavior , that is environmental attitude is a major factor in decision making vis-a-vis the consumption of " green" food and services (Jorea Ministry of Environment, 2015). Therefore, it is necessary to understand those consumer attitude, that will lead to sustainability-conductive behavior and consumption.

2.1 Environmental consumption prediction

Recently, many researchers have studied pro-environmental consumption and household indexes as well as suicide rate predictions using messages posted by internet users on Google trend, Tweets etc. channel. Whether can environmental consumption be predicted by (AI) deep-learning technological internet channel? How can impact the pro-environmental consumption attitudes of green policies? Korea scientists estimated pro-environmental attitudes using search query data provided by Google trend and confirmed through regression analysis, that pro-environmental attitude has a positive correlation with the pro-environmental attitude index. They also explained that environment-friendly attitude of residents plan an important role in policy making. In the past, most household consumption indexed were calculated through surveys, but (AI) deep-learning technological tool " big data" have recently gained research attention (Lee et al. 2016).

It seems that (AI) deep-learning technology can help agricultural export countries' farmers , e.g. US, UK, Canada, New Zealand, Australia, Japan, China, India etc. they can predict environmental behavioral consumption to any rice, tomato, potato , fruit, vegetable etc. plant food consumers. The beneficial advantages to them include as below:

(a) Assuming they know their countries' weather, when it has less rain to cause drought or when it has more rain in any seasonal time in the year. They can choose not to grow any kinds of above these plant food to avoid loss.

(b) They can make any kinds of above these plant food price raising after their prediction of these bad seasonal time to cause their plant food shortage supply challenge. Because these plant food consumers' demand number is more, but the supply of these above plant food supply number is less. However, due to they had predicted when the bad seasonal time can not allow them to grow these above plant food before. So, they have enough time to grow many these above plant food number in predictive good seasonal time to prepare to supply to their plant food import countries' plant food consumers to eat. Thus, these predictive environmental consumption plant food export countries can raise their plant food price to sell to them. When, the other non-pre-predictive environmental consumption plant food export countries can not supply any one of those plant food to them to eat, due to the bad climate to cause them can't grow any one of these plant food to export to sell.

Thus, (AI) deep-learning technology can be applied to predict how to raise the plant food supply number in order to raise price to the import plant food countries consumers to eat, due to they feel difficult to buy these plant food to eat in the bad climate seasonal time in whole year.

(c) (AI) deep-learning technology can help climate scientists to find what reasons cause their countries; rain sudden increases or cause their countries' rain sudden decreases. After its gathering data analysis, it can assist climate scientists to find solution methods to attempt to control the rain level can be right falling down level to let agricultural export farmers who can grow their plant food to sell to agricultural import countries in whole year.

(d) The agricultural export countries' farmers can apply (AI) deep-learning technology to help them to choose whether growing which kinds of plant food in that whether climate time to earn more plant food consumption number more easily.

Due to the agricultural countries climate will often change, for example, tomato, potato, rice, fruit etc. plant food can be adapt to grow in more rain time, but vegetable can not be adapt to grow in more rain time. If farmers can apply this technology to predict when it will have move rain or when it will have less rain to fall down in their countries. Then, they can choose to grow which kinds of plant food number more, in the suitable seasonal climate time in order to raise plant food growing number productivities to supply to sell to satisfy any agricultural food import countries' demand effectively.

(e) (AI) deep-learning technology can help agricultural import countries to solve agricultural food shortage challenge in long term. When this technology can be popular to base applied by the agricultural plant food export countries. It will solve global agricultural food shortage challenge. For example, when one agricultural export countries' farmers can popular accept to apply this technology to predict when to grow which kinds of plant food more to rise number productivities to sell. e.g. vegetable, fruit, rice Besides another agricultural export countries' farmers can also accept to apply this technology to predict when to grow plant food, e.g. potato, tomato to raise number productivities to sell. Then, they can concentrate on growing the specific kinds of plant food in order to raise the specific plant food number productivities in every seasonal change time every month. Then, global agricultural plant food supply must be raised, due to these predictive environmental change farmers can know who ought grow which kinds of plant food to sell to raise number productivities.

2.2 How can apply (AI) digital channel to predict consumer behaviors?

(AI) digital channel can be applied to help businesses to evaluate whether how much the product price is the most attractive to persuade consumers feel it is the most reasonable price to sell. It helps consumers to feel which brands of products which ought change the price to let consumers to choose to buy the brand of product. It can be applied to predict whether how many consumer numbers can be increased or decreased when the brand of product's price is variable. It aims to give opinions to help any brand of product manufacturers or sellers to judge whether which price is the most reasonable to let consumers to accept to choose to buy the brand of product in popular.

Thus, (AI) price measurement technology can be preference to be applied online communication ecommerce and mobile phone internet platform aspect. As businesses can enter their past products prices data and past customer number data into computer or mobile. Then, (AI) price measurement technology can gather these data to analyze these product prices and past customer number to compare their prices variable changing range level to find their price variable difference to measure to make conclusion about every product's price variable changing will influence how many customer number increase or decrease changing to choose to sell their different kinds of products more accurate. Then, (AI) price measurement software will help them to analyze all past price variable changing data to compare whether which price range can let customers to feel it is more reasonable and attractive to influence them to choose to buy the product among different brands of product choice.

Because any product's price is one important factor to influence consumers to choose to buy the product, instead of quality, durability, shape, appearance, color, brand familiarity etc. factors. Any online businesses with a focus on Asia should considerate (AI) customer care, and virtual shopping experience, whereas is Europe and North America still value face-to-face and/or real human interaction over (AI) or virtual worlds.

For example, Amazon publish has applied (AI) price measurement technology to help authors to decide how much every different topic of e-book or paper book price, it can attract the largest number of readers to buy. Any one author only needs to type whose book name to Amazon publish author himself/herself Amazon website. Amazon publish (AI) price measurement learning machine will help them to auto-calculate and judge how much e-book or paper book price is the most attractive and the most reasonable in order to increase reader number to buy their e-books or paper books to read. So, (AI) online price measurement machine will gather past similar book names and past every similar book readers' reading times and the number of readers to give opinions to let every author to judge whether his/her very new e-book or paper book ought charge how much price to the e-book or paper book which can attract many readers to choose to buy. Although, it is not ensure that the e-book or paper book price must let readers to feel it is the most reasonable price to choose to buy in reader's view point. However, it has other factors to influence readers' choice to buy the e-book or paper book, e.g. whether the book content is attractive to public, the author's familiarity, the book's page is enough or not to satisfy readers to read etc. factors. But, instead of all these extra factors to influence readers to choose to buy the book to read. (AI) price measurement learning machine can real give opinions to every author to let them to judge the e-book or paper book different price range whether is too high to influence readers to choose to buy to read or tool low to influence readers feel it is possible poor content book to compare other similar content books. Thus, (AI) price measurement machine can help authors to predict every reader's reading behaviors or reading experience and reading habit from online channel in short time easily. The author only enter the book name to let Amazon publish price measurement machine to check, it will follow past reader's reading habit and reading experience to judge whether the similar all book topic sale record to judge how much price is the reasonable price to attract many readers to buy the book.

Hence, (AI) can be applied to digital channel to help businesses to predict consumer behavior in the future. In the future, mobile/smartphone, laptop, desktop will be most frequent used ecommerce channels to develop online business. So, (AI) can be also applied to these platforms to gather data to make analysis to help businesses to predict consumer purchase behaviors popularly. Due to , ecommerce is popular to global, so digital online and instore channels can be one good channel to let (AI) learning machine to make platform to gather past every online consumer purchase (buying) experience data to help businesses to build brand personality and having a responsible, positive impact on society.

To apply (AI) learning machine technology to understand customer online purchase behavior, it will raise business e-commerce successful chance: For example, (AI) learning machine can help businesses to gather data to analyze to determine whether short-term or long-term signals in the online consumer behavior that indicate higher purchase intents to let every online business to know. (AI) learning machine can find that online users with long-term purchasing intent tend to save and click through on more content. However, as online users approach the time of purchase their activity becomes more topically focused and actions shift from saves to searches from online consumption channel. Then, (AI) learning machine will further find that the brand product purchase signals in online behavior can exist weakness before an online purchase is made and can also be traced across different online purchase categories. Finally, (AI) learning machine synthesize these insights in predictive models of online user purchasing intent to the brand of product. Taken together, it's work identifies a set of general principles and signals that can be used to model online user purchasing intent across many online content discovery applications. Thus, (AI) learning machine can help online businesses to gather any online users' click online behaviors data to judge whether there are how many online users will choose to find their online business websites to make final decisions to buy their products from online channels. Then, it will give opinions to help the online businesses to let it to judge whether what are the important website factors will help its online business to attract many online consumers, e.g. designing unattractive website issue, online unattractive product photos issue, unclear website color issue, unclear website advertisement message, contents and words impressions issue, lacking image movement frequent attractive seeing issue etc. different website factors. Thus, online digital channel will be one good choice to apply (AI) learning machine to help businesses to predict consumer behaviors.

2.3 Can apply artificial intelligent learning machine " big data" gathering method to predict manufacturers' behavioral performance ?

In consumer view point, can they apply (AI) learning machine to predict manufacturers' behavioral performance to judge whether whose products are value to buy. Nowadays, (AI) and big data are reshaping the risk in consumer privacy. For example, consumers want to hide their willingness to pay just as firms want to hide their real marginal cost, and buyers have less favorable information, say a low credit shore, prefer to withhold it just as sellers want to conceal poor product quality. So, it implies that it is possible (AI) learning machine can help customers to gather any manufacturers' past sale performance, e.g. how many complaints or appreciation from clients, product quality etc. sale data to let consumers to make judgement whether it is value to buy to compare other competitors. So, it has risk to the poor product quality of manufacturers. Otherwise, it has benefits to the good product quality of manufacturers. It also implies all manufacturers' privacy is not protected or secret when (AI) learning machine is popular to be used to predict manufacturers' behaviors by consumers.

Information economists suggest that both buyers and sells have an incentive to hide or reveal private information, and these incentives are crucial for market efficiency. Data technology that reveals consumers type could facilitate a better match between product and consumer type, and data technology that helps buyers to assess product quality could encourage high quality production.

Thus, (AI) big data technology can also assist consumers to gather different manufacturers' data to compare what their advantages and disadvantages of their products are. Then, consumers can make comparison to choose which brand of product is the suitable to whom to buy in these more choice consumption market. (AI) learning machine will gather similar brand their products' data to analyze to make conclusion to let consumers know or feel to make final judge to find what advantages or disadvantages of these sample brands of similar products' comparison from internet. On the other hand, it means that manufacturers can gather consumers' past purchase behaviors or purchase experience from (AI) big data gathering method to record and analyze to give opinions to let manufacturers to know what reasons or factors influence consumers choose not to buy their products from internet.

(AI) big data gathering consumer behavior prediction method can give these benefits to manufacturers and consumers both, such as: New concerns arise because (AI) technological advance which have enables reducing cost of collecting, storing, processing and using data in mass quantities extend information beyond a single transaction. These advances are often summarized by the big data, it means charge volume of transaction-level data that could identify individual consumers by itself or in combination with the datasets.

The popular (AI) takes big data as in input in order to understand, predict and influence consumer behavior. Modern (AI) is used by legitimate companies, could improve management efficiency motivate innovations and better match demand and supply. But (AI) in the wrong hand, also allows the mass production of fraud and deception. Since , data can be stored, traded and used long after the transaction. Future data use is likely to grow with data processing technology, such as (AI) big data gathering consumer and manufacturer behavioral prediction method from internet channel.

Thus, future (AI) big data learning machine can also help consumers to choose the best brand of manufacturer's products among different brands of manufacturers products choice to compare their past sale performance from internet. They can apply (AI) big data statistic method to gather all different manufacturers' similar products past sale data to compare their advantages and disadvantages to make the best decision to choose to buy which brand of product is the most suitable to them to buy to use. It seems (AI) big data can also help consumers to predict any manufacturers' manufacturing behaviors or manufacturing performance whether they are improving their product quality or are deteriorating their product quality. Thus, (AI) big data tool is also important to help customers to predict future the different brands of manufacturer performance will have improvement in possible.

Thus, I believe that artificial intelligent "big data" gathering method can be suggested to be applied to attempt to predict consumer behavioral changes in global business environment, the reasons are as below:

On the consumer's beneficial hand, Consumers can apply this method to attempt to gather any global manufacturers data to be analyzed by this artificial intelligent learning system. Then, it analyzed all the different brands of specific similar product manufacturer' data to compare what are the range of the best past manufacturing history and sale data to the group of best manufacturers, and what are the range of the better past manufacturing history and sale data, and what are the range of the good past manufacturing history and sale data, and what are the range of the common past manufacturing history and sale data. Finally, the (AI) learning system will compare all the specific similar product, e.g. mobile phone or computer, television, car etc. different kinds of specific products of global manufacturers to conclude the result is such as whether which brands will be the best manufacturers to let the consumer to buy the television or mobile phone or computer or car etc. different kinds of products. It can make more accurate judgement to compare general human's phone or questionnaire surveys investigation method, newspapers, television, radios, internet searches etc. different manufacturing news or data gathering channels to find which brands are the most worth confidence to consumers to choose to buy the specific product in the global consumption market.

On the manufacturers' beneficial hand, manufacturers can apply (AI) data gathering method to predict consumer emotion and buying behavioral changes more accurate. For example, the vehicle manufacturer, it plans to gather data to predict potential driving fast speed sport vehicle consumers' preferences trends in order to make the accurate judgement how to design its sport vehicles to attract many sport vehicle buyers who will choose to buy it's brand of any driving fast speed sport vehicles. It can attempt to apply (AI) intelligent learning system to gather global different brands of sport vehicle data concerns that all past driving fast speed sport vehicle buyer's preference of sport vehicle design. Then, the (AI) intelligent learning system gather global different brands of driving fast speed sport vehicle which had ever been purchased by the different country's driving fast speed sport vehicles consumers. After, it can compare divide the range of similar driving fast speed sport vehicle design and similar price to be different groups. The (AI) intelligent learning system can attempt to follow the past number of different brands of driving fast speed sport vehicle buyers to calculate how many driving fast speed sport vehicle buyers who choose to buy the brand of driving fast speed sport vehicle as well as it will analyze and make judgement to find whether the cheaper price reason attracts the different countries sport vehicle buyers choose to buy the brand of driving fast speed sport vehicle or the attractive design reason attracts the different countries sport vehicle buyers choose to buy the brand of sport vehicle or fast speed reason attracts the sport vehicle buyers choose to buy the brand of sport vehicle.

For example, although some brands of driving fast speed sport vehicle manufacturers' prices are very high, but they can still attract global many sport vehicle consumers to buy. Whether all sport vehicle's attractive design is the main factor to influence them to buy or whether it's fast speed is the main factor to influence them to buy or whether it's safe confidence it the main factor to influence them to buy or it's familiarity brand is the main factor to influence them to buy. (AI) intelligent learning system will attempt to make judgement and analysis to conclude whether the attractive design factor is the main factor to influence many sport vehicle consumers to choose to buy the brand of sport vehicles.

Otherwise, for another example, although some brands of driving fast speed sport vehicle manufacturer's prices are low, but they can not still attract many global many sport vehicle consumers to buy. Whether all vehicle's unattractive design is the main factor to influence them choose not to buy their fast speed driving sport vehicles or whether the unsafe factor is the main factor to influence them choose not to buy their fast speed driving sport vehicles or whether unfamiliarity brand is the main factor to influence many consumers choose not to buy their fast speeding sport vehicles.

Thus, when (AI) learning system had helped the fast speed sport vehicles manufacturer to gather all different brands of fast speed driving sport vehicle's past sale data and price data, design of different sport vehicle, e.g. color choice, method of style, comfortable chair styles and chair sizes and what kinds of steel material to manufacture the sport vehicles data and driving safe and accident occurrence data and the data concerns what reasons of the past complaint to brand of sport vehicle manufacturer from its sport vehicle buyers. Then, it can make more conclusion to give more accurate opinions whether which brands of fast speed driving sport vehicle manufacturer(s) whose sport vehicle design is the main factor to attract consumers choose to buy its any driving fast speed sport vehicle products really. Thus, it seems that it can make more accurate judgement to compare television survey, questionnaire survey to gather data concerns how to design the fast speed sport vehicle to attract consumers to choose to buy the sport vehicle manufacturer's planning sport vehicle products. I believe that (AI) learning system can help the sport vehicle manufacturer to make more accurate conclusion or judgement how to design its fast speed driving sport vehicles to attract it's consumers more easily.

CHAPTER THREE

AI predicts customer emotion

(AI) tool predicts consumer immediate and expected emotion how to influence consumption decision

If (AI) tool can be confirmed to apply to predict consumer behavior, then I can conclude that it can be attempted to apply to predict what the factor(s) of the product itself can cause the consumer has positive or negative emotion, so the manufacturer can attempt to avoid the bad factors cause to bring negative emotion to influence the consumer chooses not to buy the product more easily, such as vehicle product case.

Economists refer to the consumption desirability is as " utility" and the product or service consumption decision making is arose

influenced by maximizing utility only. However, they neglect consumer individual immediate emotion change will also influence the consumer individual consumption decision consequently. Expected emotions are those that are anticipated to occur as a result of the outcomes associated

with different possible courses of action. For example, if a potential investor, were deciding whether to purchase a stock, who might imagine the disappointment who would feel if who ought it and it reduced its price. Otherwise, whose emotion would experience , such as regret if it increased in price, but who does not buy it before the stock rise its price. However, I believe nowadays technology, in the future one day, (AI) tool can be attempted to assist consumer psychology profession or marketing research profession to assist them to find what are the bad factors to influence consumers choose not to buy any manufacturers' products. Then, when the manufacturer

can discover what are the bad factor(S) cause(S) consumers who do not choose to buy their products, then the manufacturer can raise whose product of consumption desirability or " utility" to raise whose product's consumption decision making is influenced by maximizing utility. Hence,

(AI) tool will be possible to find what the bad factor(S) to cause consumers do not choose to buy the manufacturer's product in order to raise the product's utility to bring consumer positive emotion to choose to buy its product in possible. SO, (AI) tool will be one consumer psychological emotion prediction tool to assist any manufacturers

to help their products to build positive emotion to any consumers in possible.

The key feature of expected emotions is that they are experienced when the outcomes of a decision materialize, but not at the moment of choice, at the moment of choice, they are only feel about future emotion. Such as consumption case, if the consumer chose to buy the product or consume the service before it's price is increased. Then, the consumer will feel happy and it is worth to purchase or consumer the service as well as the consumer's expected emotion is positive before who decides to buy the product or consume the service, because who believes or feels the product or service's price will be raised in short term, e.g. after one month, one week. Thus, it means that if the consumer does not believe or

feel or predict the product or service's price either it will increase or decrease in short term, whose emotion will be negative, those negative emotion will influence who does not decide to buy the product or service, it is possible that who feel it is not worth to buy the product or consume the service immediately. He She will choose to consume the service or buy the product to wait it's price is decreased later. it seems that the consumer's positive or negative emotion will influence who decides to buy the product or consume the service later or earlier. Thus, it has close relationship between the consumer individual immediate purchase or consumption decision and positive emotion or negative emotion (either expected emotion or immediate emotion influences).

Consequently, if (AI) tool can help any manufacturers

to predict when its product price ought to be increased or decreased in order to attract consumer to choose to buy its product. Then, it can help any manufacturers to build positive expected emotion to attract consumers to choose to buy its product more easily. For example, when the (AI) tool can predict when the consumer expects the product price will fall down, then it can give ideas to the manufacturer to raise up the product price in the month, then it predicts many consumers expect the product price will fall down after six months. So, the product price will not be fall down after six months. So, many consumers will feel disappointment and they will choose to buy the product if the manufacturer

decided to raise the product price after six months. Then, the higher product price will cause many consumers worry about the product price will continue rise up, so they will prefer to choose to buy the product immediately after six months because they afraid the product price will continue to rise up in the year. Then, I assume that (AI) tool has effort to predict when consumers feel the product will rise up or fall down, then it can give ideas to the manufacturer when to rise up or fall down the product price in order to attract or persuade many consumers choose to buy the product in different period in the year.

1.1 What does (AI) tool predict immediate emotion mean?

Psychologists indicate that immediate emotions, by contrast, are experienced at the moment of choice and fall into one of two categories. Integral emotion, like expected emotions, arise from thinking about the consequences of one's decision, but " integral emotion", unlike expected emotions are experienced at the moment of choice. Such as purchase stock case, the share buyer might experience immediate fear at the thought of the stock's losing value. " Incidental emotions" are also experienced at the moment of choice, such as a consumer predicts the product or service price whether it will be risen up or fallen down. If he/she feels the product or service price will fall down after next month and he/she will choose to buy the product or consume the service. But consequently, after next month, the product or service's price won't fall down absolutely.

Then, he/she will have incidental emotion to influence whom to choose whether he/she ought buy the product or consume the service, due to the product or service price is not still fall down. Otherwise, he/she is fear the product or service will not fall down in short term. Even, it will increase price later. Hence, whose incidental emotion will have possible to influence whom to choose to buy the product or consume the service after one month, if the product or service's price is still not increased absolutely. So, (AI) tool can be attempted to apply to predict when the product price ought need to be raised or fallen down in order to attract consumers to choose to buy the manufacturers' product in different period.

Economists indicate utility an individual consumption with an outcome might arise from a prediction of emotion: For example, a dinner eater might choose a higher utility to an Italian restaurant dinner than a French restaurant dinner because who anticipates being happier at the former, even the former's dinner price is higher than the French restaurant.

So, such as this restaurant dinner case, if one (AI) tool can assist the French restaurant owner to find what factor(S) cause(S) the dinner consumers do not choose to go to its restaurant to eat its food, e.g. high price factor, bad taste factor, bad wait service performance factor, bad cooker's cooking skill factor, poor advertisement promotion factor, poor familiar factor, poor location or poor eating environment etc. different factors. Then, the French restaurant owner can find methods to avoid the bad factor(S) cause(S) many dinner consumers do not choose to go to whose French restaurant to eat dinner more easily.

The question is that whether the positive emotion factor can influence the consumer changes whose mind to choose to consume the more expensive service or buy the more expensive product. To answer this question. it depends on whether the consumer has an imperfect understanding of whose own tastes or the consumer has a perfect understanding of whose own tastes to the product or the service.

It means the consumer will choose to buy the product or consume the service, even it's price is higher than other general similar products or services if who has a perfect understanding of whose own tastes to the product or service. Otherwise, who won't choose to buy the product or consume the service, due to it's price is higher than other general similar products or services if who has an imperfect understanding of whose own tastes to the product or service. So, it seems that the consumer's negative or positive emotion arise will be influenced by whose perfect or imperfect understanding of whose own tastes to the product or service factor.

It concludes that whether how much degree of the consumer's utility to the product or service. It is not the only one important factor to influence the consumer to choose to buy the product or consume the service. Otherwise, the consumer's imperfect or perfect understanding own tastes to the product or service factor will influence the consumer to arise positive or negative emotion to make final purchase or consumption decision immediately. It will be one more consumption influential factor to lead the consumer to make the final consumption decision making immediately. So, future (AI) tool ought to be innovate to own how to judge good taste or bad taste for any food in order to predict food consumers to choose to buy the food manufacturer's any foods more attractively.

CHAPTER FOUR

(AI) tool technical innovation in cruise tourism immediate positive emotion influence to cruise travelling consumers

Can apply (AI) tool to cause positive emotion to cruise tourism consumers? Cruise tourism industry is the most influential emotion industry example to influence cruise travelling consumers' travelling entertainment choice. I shall indicate some evidences how it's innovation will influence cruise travelling consumers' emotion to be changed to positive from negative immediately as well as to prove how the cruise traveler higher utility feeling to the cruise tourism provider is not the main factor to influence whom to choose the cruise provider to consume whose cruise journey service arrangement.

Nowadays, cruising has become one of the fastest growing sectors within tourism, cruise service providers need have themselves unique different entertainment service arrangement to satisfy every cruise travelling consumer individual needs in order to attract every one to choose whose cruise arrangement easily, e.g. meals, activities, entertainment and varied destinations create one-stop holiday shop, reasonable competitive ticket fare. Hence, it seems it is one exciting emotion industry. If the cruise service provider can bring positive emotion to influence many cruise travelling consumers immediately. The, even it change higher service fare to compare other similar cruise service providers. I believe it won't influence them to choose other similar cruise service providers if it can often bring immediate positive emotion to its cruise clients during they are staying in its cruises or during they have left its cruises, but they will often remember or won't forget to enjoy their cruise service provider's happing time forever. Hence, if (AI) tool can be attempted to help cruise entertainment providers to arrange different cruise journeys for varied destinations , to arrange different entertainment facilities, to arrange the different taste food to satisfy different countries age cruise consumers' needs. Then, the (AI) tool will assist the cruise providers to bring positive emotion to let every different countries age cruise consumers to feel satisfactory in order to choose to the cruise providers' cruise entertainment service more attractively.

2.1 How can apply (AI) tool to predict cruise service providers bring positive emotion to their clients?

Future, (AI) tool can help any cruise providers to design these kinds of any one entertainment service arrangement to satisfy the cruise provider's customers' needs.

There are different special interests cruising , such as wellness at sea, freighter cruises, river cruises. It has increased the attractiveness of cruising: Romance is for lover cruise traveler target, luxury is for rich cruise traveler target, exotica is for enjoyment exciting feeling traveler target. So, every kind of cruise traveler target will have different kind of cruise entertainment service to satisfy their needs. If the cruise service provider can provide the right and attractive cruise entertainment service to satisfy the specific cruise target. Then, it will bring the positive emotion to the specific cruise target consumers more easily.

Cruise travel was shaped for mass tourism. Prices have been very differently segmented. There are basically four types of markets (Biederman, 2008):

● Contemporary market: On board fun and amenities are playing important role and destinations have secondary importance.

● Premium market: This category is more expensive than the contemporary category and where the destination has same importance as on board amenities.

● Luxury market: It was once dominant type of cruise tourism, but now it has only a small portion of the industry. Generally, it is the most expensive cruise category and usually it takes longer than average cruise days.

● Adventure/exploration: It refers relatively long cruises with special and exotic places where the destination is the main purpose of the trip.

● European cruise travel: Duration takes more five days than worth

American travel duration. There is a tendency on European market during the years that duration of travel is getting shorter. This short demand of is explained with the strong demand of customers (Hensen, 2003). Beside this, it is most likely that cruise companies try to convince tourists with short haul travels instead of long term cruise trips for more expenditure.

Thus, I believe that even, the cruise service provider charges higher ticket which won't influence cruise consumers who do not choose its entertainment service on its cruises. If it can arrange the attractive cruise entertainment facilities and destination journey arrangement, staying days arrangement to satisfy different specific cruise target market needs absolutely in order to bring whose emotion to be positive to it's service provision. Then, the cruise service provider will attract many potential cruise clients to choose its cruise service absolutely. Otherwise, if it only bring negative emotion to its cruise clients, it will not attract many potential cruise clients to choose it or loses its old cruise clients, even, its cruise ticket price is needed to decreased in order to raise competitive effort.

In conclusion, I believe that future (AI) tools need to learn how to bring cruise consumers to arise individual immediate or expected positive emotion, this positive emotion consideration is more important to compare to how to reduce cruise ticket price in order to attract cruise clients in global cruise competitive cruise industry.

2.2 Differentiation through the characteristics of cruising route method from (AI) tool route judgement

Future, (AI) tool can attempt to help any cruise entertainment service providers to judge how to design different route to attract different countries age cruise clients' choices to satisfy their cruise journey entertainment needs. The determinants of the cruising route's characteristics (functional, social, and emotion) is important factor to influence the cruise service provider's success. Cruising product is no longer selected primarily for the cruising service, but for the content of cruising route. So, the cruising route will influence the cruise consumer individual emotion, because it is the main service need for every cruise consumer.

The approach called the " land sea cruising in product development" is increasingly becoming an area of interest, e.g. determining the direction of the effects of the individual cruising route characteristics on service value's perception , and providing an evaluation model of the route's perception , and indicating significance variables of attraction.

The questions that cruise planners need to know: How does each of the identified determinants affect the overall perceived value of the cruise route? How the overall perceived value of the cruise route affects customer behavior intentions?

Because different routes factor will influence cruise consumer individual emotion changing seriously. It means the ship has become only a tool, when the offered route whose attractiveness highly influences the impression of the guests has become crucial.

Consumer behavior in cruising segment includes all the activities and influences in the selection of the specific cruise route. There activities result in decisions and actions related to a defined price, selection and reselection of cruising company (Cannot, Brink and Brijball, 2006).

2.3 How to apply (AI) tool to arrange cruise route planning have close relationship to influence cruise consumer emotion?

Firstly, use value of cruising routes is based on the subjective experience, and shows how individuals assess the route during, or immediately after sailing. It is affiliated with the benefits that cruising guest realize by choosing a route , and it is subjective because it depends on the individual assessment (photo taken on the route for one guest presents just a family souvenir, and for professional photographers are embodied financial capital).

Secondly, the utilitarian value is also subjective-oriented and is tied on the point where the inner and us ability of cruising routes are compared with the sacrifice of the client (money and time). Finally, the value is considered as the outcome of the comparison of scarifies and personal benefits, which is resulted in essentially utilitarian nature.

Hence, route design is the main value of cruising tourism and it is primarily determined and analyzed from the aspect of observed customers. Otherwise, the cruise is only one tool to be caught for the cruise passengers, whether the cruise can let whom to sleep comfortable , providing what kind of food to them to eat, what kind of entertainment facilities are provided to them to play, these issues are not more important to compare how to design route to bring them to travel to anywhere to enjoy in this cruise journey factor. Because how to design the route factor can bring each cruise passenger to influence them to feel either negative or positive emotion directly. The whole route journey planning is the most influential factor to influence the cruise passengers to feel whether they ought choose it's service again or not in the f

(AI) tool judges the difference between utility factor and emotion to influence consumer decision making

In economic utility or immediate (expected) emotion aspects, whether which is more influential to excite consumption. To analyze whether it is economic utility or immediate (expected) emotion more influential to excite consumption. It depends on the consumer individual consumption choice is in which situations. For example, if the industry's general consumer individual consumption decision is concentrate on emotion influential aspect, such as cruise entertainment industry, hospital care service industry, theme park entertainment industry, movie watching entertainment industry etc. Above all these industries have same nature, it is service. So, it seems that service industry's main influential factor is immediate (expected) emotion influence, it is not economic utility influence. Otherwise, product sale industry's main influential factor is utility.

3.1 (AI) judges consumer utility factor

For this toy choice situation example, parent choose to buy one toy to give whose child to play. They usually considerate which kind of toy is attractive to their child whom like to play. In many different kinds of toys choice, if the child likes to choose the kind of toy to play. After the child's parents had purchased the kind of toy to let whose child to play one period time, e.g. six month. Then, when the child feel that who has need to buy another new toy to play, due to he/she feels bored to play this toy. So, it seems that the child feels this toy has less utility or it's utility is decreased. So, he/she expects whose parent can buy another new kind of toy to let whom to play. It also implies that it is not emotion factor to influence the child to feel boredom and unfunny to play this kind of old toy after six months. It is the product's utility factor which can not attract the child to play it any more. So, this old toy's utility is decreased when this child spends six months to play it. This toy's value is only six month utility to this child to play. Otherwise, if this kind of toy is bought by another parent. It is possible that the another child like to play this kind of toy one year or more. So, it's utility to another child is one year or more period. So, product's utility period is difference, it depends on how long time of the user's satisfactory time.

As this toy case, the child's decision will influence whose parent choose which kind of toy to buy to whom to play. Usually toy price is not difference too much. Parent won't consider when the toy price will be increase or will be decreased to influence their emotion to decide not to buy the toy immediately. So, when the child like to play the kind of toy, even the product's price is more than other kind of toys, and the parent feel it is possible that the kind of toy's price will be fallen down later. They will still choose to buy the kind of toy to let their child to play, they won't be influenced not to buy this kind product by later cheap price factor. So, immediate emotion is not the main factor to influence this parent does not choose buy this toy at this moment. Otherwise, utility factor will influence when the parent will buy another new kind of toy to provide to this child to play. If the child enjoy to play it only three months, after he/she will feel bore and he/she will tell whose parent to buy another new kind of toy to let whom play when the fourth month is beginning. So, it implies that if the kind of toy product can have more attractive utility time, then it can attract many parent to choose to buy it among different kind of toys. Thus, when this kind of toy's utility time is longer time. Then, it is possible that it can influence many parents choose to buy it's different style or design of similar kind of toys to let their children to play. In general, when many parents accept to buy this kind of different style or design of similar toys to give their children to play. Due to it's popular long time utility factor, it will influence children like to play it longer time to compare other kind of toys. Consequently, it will influence parents do not need often spend too much money to buy other kinds of toys to give their children to play. So, longer time utility factor to the product can attract many consumers to choose to buy the kind of product to compare lesser time utility factor to the product. Hence, it proves the explanation why utility factor is the main influential factor to influence the consumer choose to buy the product.

3.2 (AI) judgement tool of Medical care and utility case

Medical care is an input in producing health, it is subject to law of diminishing marginal productivity. Health yields utility to the consumer. It is subject to law of diminishing marginal utility. It bring this question: Does either the patient's emotion or the medical care service or medical care product utility which one can influence the patient's hospital choice more?

To answer this question: We need to know medical care is one kind of nursing care service in hospitals or clinics and medical care product is one kind of medical care product sale from merchants, e.g. medicine or medical equipment. So, in medical industry which has different kind of medical care services to provide to patients in hospitals or clinics as well as which has different kind of medical care products sale, e.g. medicine or wheelchairs, heart health measurement equipment etc. different medical care products in medical health industry.

In medical care aspect, it is one kind of any medical care service to patients from hospitals or clinics. So, medical care is an input in producing health service to patients from hospitals or clinics. When the patient is admitting to hospital or clinic, who needs to see doctor and the doctor need to give the right medicine to the patient to eat to ill whose illness. Even, if the doctor feels the patient whom needs to live hospital for one time period. Then, the hospital nurses must need to take care the patient during he/she is living in the hospital period. Consequently, if the patent can be health in short time, e.g. within one week leaving time, then he/she will be shortened time to leave the hospital in next weak. Otherwise, if the patent can not be health in short time, e.g. within on week, then he/she needs to live the hospital more than one week, even, one month, three months or more. So, the staying hospital time will influence the patent's emotion to feel whether the doctor's effort. If he/she needs to live the hospital long time, he/she will bring negative emotion to feel the doctor's medical effort is not good. The doctor's medical effort can not achieve or satisfy whose expected emotion during whose staying hospital time.

Thus, medical care is an input service in producing health, it is subject to law of diminishing marginal productivity. When the patient does not need to live the hospital longer time, the patient will feel more satisfactory to the hospital's doctor and nurses' care effort as well as the patient can give less money to spend the expenditure to live the hospital. So, the law of diminishing marginal health productivity will explain the hospital will shorten time to the staying days of the hospital to the patent as well as the patient's care expenditure will be decreased when he/she only needs to live to the hospital in short time. Otherwise, the patient needs to live longer time in the hospital, it means that the diminishing marginal health productivity to the hospital, the patient's staying hospital days will be increased and the patient's medical expenditure to the hospital will also be increased. It will bring negative emotion to patient and why this negative emotion factor will influence the patient would choose another hospital to live or find other doctors to see if he/she felt illness in future one day.

In medical care product aspect, health yields utility to the consumer. It is subject to law of diminishing marginal utility. Because patient needs to buy different kind of medical equipment to use or medicine to eat to attempt to cure whose illnesses. So, if the patent can choose the right medicine to eat from the doctor's recommendation or if the patent can choose the right medical equipment to use from the doctor's recommendation. When the patient buy less number of medicine to eat, then he/she can be health or when he/she buy the medical equipment to use, then he/she can be health. Then, he/she will spend less money to buy medicine to eat or medical equipment to use and he/she can be health in short time. Then, the medical consumer will feel the medicine or medical equipment has good utility to satisfy whose medical needs. So, good medicine and good medical equipment can only need short time and less money to let the medical patient to be health.

3.3 Immediate (expected) emotion factor

As cruise entertainment case, every cruise journey must provide fixed stay days on the cruise to let every cruise passenger to play to every cruise journey. So, cruise passenger can not change or extend whose fixed stay day choice in every cruise journey, when they had caught the cruise to go to sea on the day. Is implies that cruise entertainment has none longer time utility factor which can influence each cruise passenger's choice to each different design of cruise journey arrangement.

If the cruise passenger feels very satisfactory and enjoyable to the last time of specific cruise journey arrangement, e.g. five days and four nights New Zealand and Australia cruise journey. Due to this cruise journey can bring positive emotion to let the cruise passenger to let whom feel that he/ she can not forget or remember this happy cruise journey forever.

It is possible that this time happy five days and four nights New Zealand and Australia cruise journey will bring positive emotion to influence this cruise passenger to choose to find this cruise service provider to help whom to arrange this same cruise journey or another similar cruise journey again after one month, or three month, or six month or one year or more. Due to this cruse passenger felt this cruise service providers' cruise journey design arrangement can satisfy whose needs and it can achieve whose expected emotion to be positive. So, this cruise entertainment industry must be immediate (expected) emotion influential factor more than time utility factor to influence the cruise consumer's cruise service provider and cruise journey choices.

In conclusion, it is not only utility factor can influence consumption decision. It is emotion factor can also influence consumption decision. It depends on situations whether the consumer is choosing to buy one product or consume one service. If the consumer is choosing to buy one product, how long time of the product's utility factor which will influence the consumer choose to buy which product. If the consumer feels the product can give longer utility time among other similar products, then he/ she will have more chance to choose to buy the product. Otherwise, if the consumer feels the product can give lesser utility time among other similar products, then he/she will have less chance to choose to buy the product. If the consumer is choosing to consume one service, emotion factor will influence the consumer choose to find which service provider to consume the same service or similar service. If the service provider can provide excellent service to the consumer, then it will bring positive immediate or expected emotion to whom and it can attract the consumer to choose the service provider again. Otherwise, if the service provider can not provide excellent service to the consumer, then will bring negative immediate or expected emotion to whom and it can not attract the consumer to choose the service provider again.

CHAPTER SIX

Why and how (AI) judgement tool can judgement what utility factors are to influence consumer emotion

In emotion and utility both aspects, they include these situations. I shall explain how and why emotion and utility factors can influence consumption behaviors in these different situations as below:

(1) In the first situation is brand factor, the brand image, product quality, product knowledge , attitude and

(2) brand loyalty intangible factor will attract the consumer individual purchase.

For example, luxury

products, e.g. luxury fashion brands of clothing. Brands like Zara from Spain and H&M from Seweden began to produce catwalk-style fashion at low cost offering consumers of luxury fashion alternatives at low prices.

Nowadays, the luxury fashion sector is the fourth largest revenue generator in France, and one of the most remarkable sectors in Italy, Spain , the USA and the potential markets of China, Russia and India. The luxury industry has increased having a huge youth in demand. The luxury consumer have much choice in products, shopping channels and pricing of luxury products. It has possible relationship of age, gender, income and other demographic factors with purchasing intentions to influence the rational and emotional buying behavior regarding luxury fashion products.

(2) The second situation concerns the decision-making of make or female consumers are possible experience an emotional desires and cognitive (reasoning) mind in purchasing choice process. Their emotion includes negative or positive buying emotion and mood management and cognitive process components include cognitive deliberation, planning buying with the exception regard for the future.

University had been using analysis of variances tests, male and female students were found significantly different with respect
affective process components including positive buying emotion, and mood management and cognitive process components include planning buying.

Significant differences were also found between the following product categories: shirts/sweaters, skirts, coats, underwear, accessories, shoes, electronic hardware, computer software, music , CD or DVDs, sports, memorabilia, health /beauty products and magazines/books for pleasure reading. No differences were found in regard to suits/business wear and entertainments.

The investigate proved that some products will have different emotion influence to cause female or male students whose final consumption decision to buy the kind of product. So, the difference od male and female students will have emotion influence to make purchase decision to buy the product in consuming choice process.

(3) The third situation concerns search advertising factor, e.g. online search to influence consumption behavior. Advertising is possible one method to persuade the consumer to choose to buy the product, even the consumer does not know the product exists. For example, proper cloth, a company based in New York, has a site on the social networking site Facebook.

Whenever the company posts a new photos of its clothes, all its face book " fans" automatically receive the information on their own face book pages. "We want to hear what our customers have to say." It seems online advertisement is a potential promotion method to promote any new attractive products to sell to let publicity to know to buy. Internet is one popular communication tool to be used by youth today. So, when one company can have one website to let any youth to find and enter to the website to discover any new things easily. It will cause many consumption chances to let online potential clients to attempt to choose any products to make purchase decision from online advertising tool easily.

How does the role of advertising influence the purchase decision process? Needs and motivations are the starting points of purchase decisions. In fact, advertising is a communication of photo image, sound image, and word advertisement image channel to persuade consumers to choose to buy the brand of product or consume the brand of service between the merchant and its consumers from television, radio, newspapers, magazine, movie etc. channels.

Why does advertisement influence consumer
choice? For this case example, when one buyer waits until more information is gathered before making a decision. The time, two types of cost are involved. First, there are psychological opportunity costs experienced by consumers who are deprived of the product who need and are consequently in a state of psychological tension.

As time elapses, this psychological tension becomes more frustration. Second, buyers experience costs with the information-gathering efforts. They must invest time and energy to visit several retailers, seek out and read advertisements, or inquire for other opinions about the best product to buy.

These delayed decision costs considerably increase as time elapses. The buyer must seek information until it is felt that a search for additional information will bring about more costs than benefits. So, an advertisement is reaching a potential buyer when who is seeking information will have a greater impact, since the buyer is spending time and effort needed to seek out this information himself and he is less likely to find other competing and advertisements to obtain the additional information.

In general, buyers are generally more responsive to different brand advertisements, when they are seeking information on these brands. This is why the becomes a choice target for the advertiser provided the advertiser can identify and locate them. Thus, a client has interested and is in an information-gathering stage is asked.

Then, the advertiser takes advantage of the consumer's having identified him or herself to send a series of informative and persuasive messages or to send a salesperson who will try to conclude a sale. Thus, advertisement gives a chance to let consumers to gather information to choose the best product to buy or the most excellent service to consume.

What of situations do merchants need advertisements promotion? The short purchase cycle markets are characterized by routine
purchase decision processes or by limited problem solving when a new brand is introduced on the market, e.g. coffee, bread , sugar, soft drinks, canned vegetables and household and beauty care products fall into this category. Another irregular purchase cycle markets are characterized by products that are purchased more or less regularly , e.g. cookies, cake mixes, wines, food products. Finally, long or unpredictable purchase cycle markets include all durable products, such as cars, household appliances and furniture (products from which occasions of purchase can't be predicted, which most consumers buy only occasionally). Hence, these kinds of products ought need advertisement promotion specially, due to advertisement can build brand image to let consumers to know. Especially , it is a new brand of product. In conclusion, advertisement will be one good channel to let new product to introduce its brand to let clients to remember in minds heart.

Consequently, future (AI) tool needs to learn how to design different kinds of advertisement to attract consumer attention to the product, needs to learn how to find what the bad factor(S) which cause(S) many consumers do not choose to buy the product, needs to learn when the product price needs to be raised up or fallen down in order to bring consumers' positive emotion to choose to buy the product immediately. SO, if (AI) tool can be invented to own itself effort to design different kinds of methods to predict consumer behavior in order to bring their positive emotion to the product successfully, then the manufacturer can earn positive consumer emotion advantage from the (AI) tool assistance for long term benefit to its product.

4.1 (AI) digital data gather technology predicts food consumer behavior's main barriers

What are the main barriers to food industry? When the food manufacturer applies (AI) big data gather technology to predict food consumer behavior? The barriers include that the food manufacturer / provider needs to decide whether when the right time is applied to the right (AI) digital big data prediction tool channel to find the right food consumers to be chose to full food consumption satisfactory questionnaires, how to gather multi-class food consumption classifiers on real-world food consumers transactional data from the food sale domain consistently to show the critical numbers of different kinds of food items at which the predictive performance most accurate? So, any food manufacturer /

provider's advanced in (AI) digital data gather warehousing and management technologies can provide that opportunities for food business to enhance long term relationship with the food providers' clients.

However, food industry's (AI) digital data gather aims to improve food customer product targeting, increase food customer loyalty and food purchase probability to the food supplier. To effective identify, understand and satisfy the needs of their food customers, the food suppliers need to develop the right (AI) digital questionnaire questions and find the right food customers to fill every right questions from every digital questionnaire at the right time through the right channel.

Above of all these, they will be the barriers when one food supplier expects its (AI) digital data gather questionnaires which can conclude the most accurate prediction concerns any kinds of consumer food product choices. So, such as (AI) digital data prediction model, it is needed to incorporate into the food market segmentation, food customer targeting, and food challenging decisions with the goal of maximizing the total food customer lifetime. For example, (AI) big data gather transaction data is reasonable and accurate for building predictive models. Transaction data can be electronically collected and readily made available for data mining in lot quantity at minimum extra costs.

Suggestion to apply (AI) prototypes of food customer profiles method to predict food customer behavioral changes. Prototypes of food customer profiles mean to be extracted from the discovered bins and multi-class classifies models are built using those prototypes. The learned models can than be used to predict the class of food customer profiles (e.g. restaurants, school canteens, supermarkets etc. food suppliers) based on their food purchases. The approach is validated on the case study of a food retail and food service company operating in food and beverages market.

So, a food customer profile, it is a description (AI) data gather tool will record every of food customer using available information, which help in understanding their background and food consumption behavior. (AI) data gather tool can well develop every food customer profile, every food customer data is essential in food market analysis as they aid food suppliers in saving time and money by highlighting the real potential food consumers whose needs are to be met rather a range of individuals.

So, (AI) data gather tool can record every food consumer profile and every can be factual or behavioral food consumption. A factual food customer profile consists of a set of characteristics for (AI) big data gather record, e.g. demographic information , such as food customer name, gender, birth date, when a behavioral food customer profile consists of what the food customer is actually doing and is usually derived from (AI) digital transactional data gather record.

So, (AI) big data gather record's every behavioral food consumer profile can be much stronger predictor of the future food supplier consumption choice actions of a food customer. Furthermore, the food supplier's (AI) all past food consumer information that make up demographically based all past food customer profiles are expensive to acquire when the information for the food suppliers' past every food consumer food consumption behaviors. Moreover, food customer profile can be recorded to make real food purchase every time. So, when the food supplier finds the past food consumer's record from (AI) big data gather tool. Then, it can make more accurate judgement whether past every food consumer has chose to buy its food to eat how many times every year in order to predict whether its every past food consumer will choose to buy its foods how many times next year in possible. If the next year, its every past food consumer's consumption time to the food supplier is less than its current year consumption time. Then, the food supplier can attempt to find whether what factors to cause the past food consumers do not choose to increase food purchase times to the food supplier in current year. The factors may be possible be the food supplier's food prices are raised, food quality or taste is poor, the different kinds of food supply is shortage challenge, the food supplier's consumers lose confidence to buy the food supplier's foods to eat, when (AI) big data gather tool can help the food suppliers to find what the main factors to cause the past food consumer number to be reduced in order to predict how future food consumers' behavioral changes will be influenced from the food supplier's competitors in the global food supply market. Hence, (AI) big data gather tool can help every food supplier to attempt to find what the main factors to case the food supplier's food consumer number to be reduced as well as it can help the food supplier to predict how the food supplier's potential (past not every purchase its any food consumers) food consumers who can be persuaded to choose to buy its foods to eat by learning what the main factors influence.

In conclusion, (AI) big data gather tool can help the food supplier to find what the main factors influence its past food consumers do not choose to buy its food more times or find what the main factors will attract its potential (not ever buying its foods consumes) food consumers to choose to buy the food supplier's foods to eat.

4.2 The challenges of (AI) big data gather shaping the future of retail for consumer industries

Another challenge of (AI) big data gather is that how to shape the consumer behavior to let business owner to feel or know or predict. It means that how it express it's conclusion or opinion for every consumer behavior after it had gather all big data in any data gather period, e.g. three months, half year or one year consumer shopping model data gather period.

Because every kind of industry, consumers will continue to demand price and quality change , with a wide range of convenient fulfilment options among of different kinds of products or services supply. Overall, the (AI) big data gather procedure gives opinion concerns every time retail experience will become more exciting, simple and convenient, depending on the consumer's ever-changing needs. So, I believe that (AI) big data gather every conclusion or result will be different, due to consumer's price and quality demand will often change to every kind of product or service supply in retail industry. So, how to shape (AI) big data gathering's analytical conclusion or result more clear. I shall recommend organizations need to build great understanding of and a stronger connection to increasingly empowered consumers before they plan and implement how to apply (AI) big data gather tool to predict consumer behavior as below:

Firstly, (AI) is empowered by technology, the consumer is redefining value. The traditional measures of cost, choice and convenience are still relevant, but not control and experience are also important. Globally, consumers have access to more than 2 billion different products choice by a wide range of traditional competitors and dynamic new entrants, all experimenting with new business models and methods of client engagement.

As choice increases, loyalty becomes more difficult familiarity and the consumer becomes more empowered. Businesses will have no choice and constantly innovate and disrupt themselves by meeting new technologies of high standards and expectations of consumers. So, (AI) data gather tool will need to follow different target group of consumers' needs to follow their different kinds of product design or style choice preferable to gather data in order to conclude the different target groups of consumer behavior to give opinion more clear and accurate to let businessmen to understand more clear how its customers' behavioral choice trend in the future half month, even to two years period.

Secondly, businessmen need to adopt changing technologies rapidly. Technology will be the key driver of this retail industry. Industry participants will only success if they have a clear prediction to focus on how to using technology to increase the value added to consumers. They must , however, do so will I realistic assessment of their costs and benefits. Hence, (AI) big data gather technological tools will need to design to help them to gather data efficiently by these ways, such as the internet of things (IOT), artificial intelligence (AI) machine learning, augmented reality (AR)/virtual reality (VR), digital traceability. So, future (AI) big data gather tool are predicted to be most influential customer behavioral positive emotion changing tool for retail , due to their widespread applications , ability to drive efficiencies and impact on labor in order to impact consumer behavior changing effort from negative emotion to positive.

Thirdly, (AI) big data gather tool is an advanced data science of consumer behavior predictive tool. Businesses will have to bring the journey from simply collecting consumer data to using it to scale and systematize enhanced decision making across the entire value chain. When focused on their business goals, industry players should not lose sight of the impact that future capabilities and transformative business models may have on society.

However, (AI) big data gather tool will encounter these challenges when any business plans and implements to apply it to predict consumer behavior in retail industry. The challenges include that as below:

1. The high cost and difficulty of implementing new technologies . The (AI) big data gather tool needs capital and capabilities to be designed to implement to be applied to different retail industry users. so, expensive barriers to innovation, an organization and the skillsets of its people to support a new design of (AI) big data gather tool, highly digital technology may be required.

2. Slow pace of cultural change. Consumers need to adapt or accept (AI) new technology consumption model in the traditional retail industry. The rate of change is outpacing the ability of businesses to keep up. (AI) big data gather tool needs to be designed to adopt in new or evolved business model requires, in most cases, a new level of customer behavioral predictive machine operation will impact to influence any retail businesses' consumer behavioral changes at a minimum, an organization's structure, capabilities,

culture and decision making. If the retail business expects to apply (AI) big data gather tool to predict how to change its consumer behaviors and how their consumption behaviors will tend to change in order to achieve to change their positive emotion from negative emotion before they choose to buy its product or consume its service in success.

4.3 Challenge to using (AI) neural networks to predict customer behavior from big data gather tool

(AI) big data gather tool will encounter the challenge: How can predict customer behavior be represented as sequential data describing the interactions of the customer with a company or an (AI) data gather system through the time, e.g. these interactions are items that the customer purchase or views ? So, every customer data gather , (AI) needs to spend time to analyze how and why to cause whose consumption behavioral choice. It is too difficult matter or judgement for (AI) learning. So, (AI) needs to spend time to learn how to analyze every customer's shopping behavior or actin in order to gather all different consumers' past shopping action information in order to help business owners to predict future its potential customer shopping behavior how to change more clear and accurate prediction.

(AI) big data gather tool needs to learn to know that how to judge every customer interaction likes purchases over time can be represented with sequential data. Sequential data has the main property that the order of the information is important. Many (AI) machine learning models are not suited for sequential data, as they consider each input sample independent from previous ones. Therefore, at the end of the sequence, (AI) big data gather learn machines need to keep in their internal state of every customer purchase data, kind of product or service, price , whole year consumption times form all previous inputs, making them suitable for this type of data.

However, consumer behavior can be represented as sequential data describing the interactions through the time. Examples of these interactions are the items that the user purchases or views. Therefore, the history of interactions can be modeled as sequential data, which has the particular trial that an incorporate a temporal aspect. For example, if a user buys a new mobile phone, who might purchase accessories for this mobile phone in the near future or it the user buys a electronic book or paper book , he might be interested in books by the same author. Therefore, to make accurate predictions is important to model this temporal aspect correctly. To solve this predictive challenge of consumers to buy the product. One count the number of purchased products of a particular category in the last N days, or the number of days since the last purchase.

So, the (AI) big data gather designers can attempt to produce a feature vector which can be fed into a machine learning algorithm such as " logistic regression" will be the main feature and function to any (AI) big data gather machine to learn how to apply this " logistic regression" function or feature to predict any customer behavioral change for any product purchase or service consumption to the (AI) predictive consumer behavioral business users. Every different kinds of product purchases or services consumption will be needed to design " different model of logistic regression" in order to follow the kind of business to predict whose consumer purchase or service consumption behavior to predict more accurate.

4.4 Challenges of artificial intelligence, algorithms technology and machine learning impact to consumption market

Markets have played a key role in providing individuals and businesses with the opportunity to gain from trade. If (AI) big data gather tool can predict how to change potential customer behavior in success. The challenges to consumers will face that the overall market consumption model will be dominated by the businessmen only. So, it is not fair or reasonable to consumers, because (AI) big data gather tool has controlled or dominated all consumers' minds and it has predicted how and why every kind of product or service consumer shopping model or consumption behaviors how will change.

It will bring this questions: How can market designers learn the characteristics necessary to set optimal, or at least better, reserve prices after they had gather all data to conclude the analytical results of their consumers behaviors how will change? How can market designers better learn the environments of their markets?

In response to these challenges, artificial intelligence (AI) and machine learning are important tools for market design. For example, retailers and marketplaces , such as eBay, Amazon and many others are mining their vast amounts of data to identity patterns that help them create better shopping experiences for their clients and increase the efficiency of their markets. By having better prediction tools, these and their companies can predict and better manage dynamic consumption market environments. The improved forecasting that (AI) and machine learning algorithms provide help marketplaces and retailers better anticipate consumer demand and producer supply as well as help target products and activities for segmented markets. Another important application of (AI) 's strength in improving forecasting to help markets operate more efficiently is in electricity market example. To operate efficiently, electricity marker makers can attempt to apply (AI) machine learning tool to follow every household family electricity consumers' past electricity consumption record to judge (predict) how it will be every family's forecasting in the year.

An inaccurate forecast in the electricity supply and demand that can dramatically affect electricity market bad supply outcomes causing high variance in electricity charge prices or worse, blackouts. By better predicting every family's electricity demand and supply , electricity market makers can better allocate power generation to the most efficient power sources and maintain a more reasonable electricity stable charge market. Any example is design market, the application of (AI) algorithms to market design are already widespread and diverse.

(AI) algorithms technology , it is a safe that (AI) will play a growing role in the design and implementation of market over a wide range of applications. The challenges are that how (AI) can guarantee accurate to predict when and why and how consumer behavioral changes to any retail industries. In fact, retailers will need to discover the value that (AI) can bring to what benefits to influence their customer behaviors.

In the future, (AI) will bring their benefits to influence customers to build positive emotions to any retailers in these aspects as below:

1. Future (AI) big data gather tool will be an area of compute science that deals with giving machines , the ability to seem like they have human intelligence. In short, it is the power of a machine to copy intelligent human behavior. For example, machine learning algorithms are being integrated into analytics and customer relationship management platforms to uncover information on how to better serve customers, chat bots have been incorporated into websites to provide immediate service to customers.

2. (AI) adoption continue to rise with chat bots taking the lead. Due to increasing ease of deployment , instant availability and improved quality, chat bots will become more and more common to manage customer service queries and to make intelligent purchase recommendations. Also, retailers can engage this kind of technology to answer continue questions and

supplement customer support with chat-based shopping experience. So, (AI) and declines personalized, customized and localized experiences to customers.

(AI) will be applied across the entire retail product and service cycle, firm manufacturing to post-sale customer service interactions. Hence, retailers can use (AI) to its fullest potential will be also to influence purchases in the moment and anticipate future purchases, guiding shoppers towards the right products in a regular and highly personalized manner.

3. (AI) technology can rise the conscious customers. Customers are demanding an increased interest in the ethical practice of the brands they buy from. Todays, customers have a well-developed sense of what is solely intended to drive sales. This has lead to a rise in consumers ho make values based judgements about what to buy and where to shop. These consumers believe their purchase habits have an impact on the world. To win customers, retailers need have good conscious to predict consumers' desire. Future, (AI) data gather technology will be a good consumer behavior predictive tool to predict about for years will now become customer expectations and will have drastically changed the path to purchase. So, (AI) data gather tool is the predictive consumer expectations tool on every interaction, they have these brands.

4. Future (AI) can be impacted to influence consumer behaviors by its potential to free up time, enhance, quality, and enhance personalization. The industries include: Healthcare industry can apply (AI) to support diagnosis by detecting variations in patient data, early identification of potential pandemics, imaging diagnostics; automat industry can apply (AI) to autonomous fleets to ride sharing, semi-autonomous features, such as driver assist, engine monitoring and predictive, autonomous maintenance; financial service industry can apply (AI) to design the suitable personalized financial planning, fraud detection and anti-money laundering and automation of customer operation; transportation and logistics industry can apply (AI) to autonomous trucking and delivery, traffic control and reduced congestion and enhanced security; technology, media and telecommunications industry can apply (AI) to search media, and recommendation, customized content creation and personalized marketing and advertising to attract retailers to promote; retail and consumer industry can apply (AI) to design personalized production, anticipating customer demand, , inventory and delivery management; energy industry can apply (AI) to read and record smart metering , more efficient grid operation and

storage and predictive maintenance; manufacturing industry can apply (AI) to enhance monitoring and auto-correction of processes, supply chain and production optimization and on-demand production.

Hence, future (AI) technology will impact consumer technology when any retailers apply it to assist its manufacturing processes or product sale or service provision processes to satisfy consumers' needs, it means that it can help any retailers to influence positive emotion to consumers in their whole sale or consumption or purchase processes

5. (AI) and machine learning technologies make it possible to capture, process, and inter data on a massive scale effectively , then any human being could ever do. For example, Criteo's creative technology " Kinetic design" can apply insights from 1.2 billion monthly impressions to select and optimize individual branded advertisements components according to each shopper's preference and intent. This ensures more personalization and visually inspiring on brand ads. resulting in up to 12% more sales for (AI) technology advertiser clients.

Moreover, advertisers can now engage and inspire shoppers on a more personal level, rendering custom ads. it real-time for every impression. So, designer continues to learn from each design's success to make ads. more and more effective over time. Furthermore, brands are increasingly using paid search on retail sites to draw attention to their products on the crowded online shelf, e.g. Google shopping is a key growth area's more users are engaging with shopping ads. and across the globe. Google shopping has become essential to retailers' marketing strategies, but is a difficult channel to apply its tool to be promoted effectively . Thus, future (AI) and machine -learning technologies can dramatically improve digital commerce performance application to apply (AI) and machine learning to digital consumer. So, future (AI) technology can be applied to digital commerce aspect, it will fall into the categories of pattern recognition, classification, prediction and consumer behavior.

In conclusion, the benefits of using (AI) in digital commerce include: improved efficiency in discovering the relationships between datasets over traditional methods, which require complex modeling and coding, improved accuracy for clearly defined processes that involve a lot of manual processing, ability to deal with a large emotion of data with many attributes, for example: customer behavior data, multichannel and multi-device data , complex product data and fraud detection, more accurate analysis, such as customer segmentation sentiment, analysis and personalization frequent algorithum refreshes, such as several times a day, to capture the changes in customer and market behavior.

Finally, however, a lot of types predictive consumption behavior around (AI), in particulars that driven by vendors claiming their solutions are (AI) , ready and can deliver dramatic improvements over existing technologies. Application leaders for digital commerce can be misled into believing that (AI) can solve all their problems, which is not true for n in-depth discussion of the (AI) consumers and market behavioral predictive tool and machine -learning technologies bot. Thus, (AI) prediction consumer behavioral technology can give beneficial quantitative analysis for forecasting in business and market especially in consumer behavior and in the consumer decision-making process (consumer choice model) more effectively and efficiently.

CHAPTER SEVEN

Is Artificial Intelligent the most effective and accurate consumer behavioral tool

Is (AI) the best and the most effective and accurate consumer behavioral prediction tool to compare other kinds of consumer behavioral prediction tools? Nowadays, retailing competitions are serious businessmen often find different kinds of methods to attempt to predict consumer changes. The consumer behavioral predictive methods can include as these below methods, instead of (AI) big data gathering tool.

Firstly, statistics is the popular mathematic method, it applies auto-regression, liner regression, structural equation modelling, logistic regression statistic techniques to be used to predict consumer behaviors. Secondly, it is classification method, it sis a support vector machine to assist businessmen to make consumer behavioral prediction, it also includes decision making tress diagram technique. Thirdly, it is rule mining method, it is algorithm, market base analytic etc. business marketing concept analytical tool, it also includes graph mining technique tool. Next, it is psychological prediction model tool, it is psychology prediction model too, it is a kind of psychological method to predict consumer behaviors. Finally, it is the most updated and potential artificial neural network (ANN) machine tool, it gathered big data, then it will carry on analyzing and applies psychological method to conclude the most accurate and reasonable solutions to give recommendation to businesses to predict when and how and why their consumer behaviors will change. So, it is one owned human mind's machine and owned psychological and analytical efforts to replace humans to make any judgement in order to make the most accurate predictive behavioral changes for consumers, instead of the traditional marketing concept and psychological and mathematic methods to predict consumer behavior, (AI) big data gathering tool will be another new tool.

What are the advantages of (AI) tool to be used to predict consumer behaviors as well as what are the different between it and other traditional consumer behavioral predictive tools? I shall explain as below:

Firstly, as above all case studies are explained to (AI) questionnaire design method benefit, I believe (AI) big data gathering tool can be applied to help human to analyze and design any the suitable valid questions to enquire any kinds of business consumers in order to gather the most meaning and useful opinions to conclude the most accurate consumer behavioral prediction for every questionnaire. So, future (AI)'s analytical effort and decision making effort most be exceed above human's judgement efforts. So, future (AI) can help human to design the most useful and meaning different kinds of valid questionnaire (survey) questions as well as assist humans to analyze and make accurate decision making and conclusions to give opinions to help businessmen to predict when consumer behaviors will change and how their consumption behaviors will change to influence their businesses in order to help them to make any efficient and effective and accurate solutions to avoid consumer number to be decreased and the most important benefit is that it can give opinions to help businessmen to explain why (what the factors) cause their consumer behaviors change suddenly. It will be human's efforts can not achieve to exceed (AI)'s efforts in the future.

Secondly, (AI) can make artificial machine judgement and analytical effort, without human misleading or unfair or unreasonable judgement. So, it can make more fair and reasonable and accurate conclusion to give opinions to predict when, how and why consumer behaviors will change suddenly to the kind of business in customer model building process and evaluating the results of customer relationship management –related investment more accurate.

Furthermore, (AI) big data gathering tool will help businesses to improve the success rate of acquiring customers, increasing sales and establishing competitiveness. (AI) big data gathering tool can give opinions how to build customer loyalty to be positive emotion impact and it can find solutions to avoid every client's negative emotion causes to bring complaints behavior to the businessman's product or service. For example, Telecom industry and aggressive research has been conducted in this by applying various data mining techniques to avoid long distance phone call users' complaints. If gathered any long distance phone call users' past complaint data to record what are their general complaint issues. Then, (AI) tool will analyze all these past complaint issues to conclude and give opinions to let Telecom knows whether which aspects encounter challenge that Telecom needs to improve it's long distance phone call services or functions in order to satisfy Telecom's long distance phone call users' needs for long term. After Telecom attempted to improve its services and/ or functions from (AI) opinions and solution methods, when it fell it's long distance phone call users have positive emotions to satisfy its service performance and function performance. Then, it can prove (AI) tool's opinions and solutions are useful. The consequence is that their complain numbers will be decreased and they won't plan to choose another long distance phone call telephone service company to replace Telecom long distance phone call service more easily.

So, (AI) big data gathering tool can concentrate on finding focus on components of customer relationship management method and datasets more accurate and efficient and effective than human's data gathering and analytical effort. It implies (AI) big data gathering tool has unique more efficient and effective and accurate dataset gathering and analytical and judgement and decision making effort, it is human can not achieve.

Thirdly, (AI) big data gathering tool has much customer loyalty predictive effort. It's effort is more easily subsequently selected, reviewed and classified to compare human's gathering data effort in whole data gathering and analytical process.

In (AI) big data gathering process, (AI) can organize whole big data gathering process and technique more easily in short time. It will include these four steps. The first stage is that customer identification stage, customer identification also known as acquisition has to do with targeting the population , who are most likely to become customer segmentation. So, (AI) can help different kinds of businesses to gather their competitors' consumer purchase behavior data in short time, it is human can not achieve. The second stage is that customer attraction stage, after (AI) maker has been segmented for the business when it has ensured to gather the businessman's global competitors' consumers data. Then it analyze these all data to find solutions / methods to give the best opinions to the organizations how to achieve the direct effort and resources into attracting the target customer segments. The third stage is that customer retention, it can be defined as the activity that an organization undertakes in order to reduce customer defections. TO be successful, customer retention starts with the first contact on organization has with a customer and continues throughout the entire lifetime of a relationship involves loyalty programs, one to one marketing and complaints management. SO, (AI) can consist the business to find the best or the most reasonable , efficient , effective solutions or methods and it will conclude all these solutions to find the most reasonable and useful opinions to achieve to the aim to help the business to reduce customer complain numbers and help the business to build confident loyalty relationship between it and its clients. SO, (AI)'s analytical effort and decision making effort can be more accurate than human's analytical effort and decision making effort. IT can achieve it's consumer behavioral predictive aim more accurate and efficient and effective in the shortest time to compare human.

Fourthly, (AI) big data gathering tool can design more accurate dataset program for questionnaire (survey) to compare human's questionnaire (survey) effort. It means that (AI) can spend less time to research and make judgement what are the most reasonable and meaning questions for different kinds of businesses' needs. This includes data conduction a questionnaire, survey or interview of the individual or environment researched, public data repository: This includes commercially available public data; organizational data; this contains data collected from an organizational database, organizational information system. For example, their website log details etc. It also includes company transactional data, data purchased from a company.

For example, one vehicle sale company expects to research all global vehicle sale companies' past the different kinds of vehicle styles, design sale number data, the different kinds of vehicle style, design sale price data, every country's vehicle consumer number to the vehicle purchase number data to the vehicle company in short time. (AI) big data gathering tool can help the vehicle sale company to gather all any one for these global vehicle sale competitors' past data in the short time. It is human effort, who can not achieve this efficient, effective and accurate data gathering aim for this vehicle sale company. Even, when (AI) had gathered all global it's vehicle competitors' past sale data, (AI) can make more accurate analytical and judgement and decision making effort to design different kinds of questionnaire (survey) questions to prepare to enquire it's different target segmentation vehicle potential clients in order to predict what are their needs to choose to buy any vehicles from the vehicle company. SO, (AI) tool can conclude more accurate conclusions and give the most reasonable and useful opinions to let the vehicle company to know in order to predict what are it's potential vehicle buyer's needs and manufacture the suitable vehicle styles or designs to raise their vehicle purchase desires.

Fifthly, (AI) tool is only one perfect tool for big data gathering in order to achieve accurate results and increased profit. What is (AI) big data gathering mean? The term " big data" gathering describes the accumulation and analytical of vast amounts of information, but big data is much more than a big amount of data. It is also the ability to extract meaning to sort through big volumes of numbers and find the hidden patterns, unexpected correlations and surprising connections that can be used in different industries like medical field, security and protection field or marketing that adopt " big data driven" decision making enjoy significantly greater productivity than those that do not. So, the benefits of (AI) is given to the company by using big data repaid complexity of implementation projects and hence project risks, when accelerating time to value. It is why that human's gathering effort can not replace (A I) data gathering effort.

All analysing above benefits to (AI) big data benefits to any organizations, it brief this question: How can (AI)apply big data gathering and analysing to predict when and how any why consumer behavior will change suddenly? The purchase decision making process is consumers reducing purchase choice behaviors.

Consumers are being considered pure rational beings (consumer tried only to satisfy self-interest). Hence, due to future (AI) owns human's psychological , analytical , emotional predictive, purchasing decision making effort.

(A I) will be assumed to sees one customer how who will make purchase decisions. So, after the (AI) gathered all data concerns the find of business's past customer segmentation purchase activities, e.g. age, sex,. Income level, the product's style sale number, the product price variable sale etc. different kinds complex data.

It can make more accurate psychological and analytical effort to predict when the business's consumer behaviors will change as behaviors will change as well as find what reasons their consumption behaviors will change and how trend of their consumer behaviors will change more accurate. For example, today there are a lot of industries that use big data: healthcare (treatment) becoming personalized and patient centric and predictive analysis are used to prevent diseases for example Angelina Jolie under event a predictive double mastectomy after learning she had 87% rich to developing breast cancer, sports (by using sensors data are collected from players during a game in order to improve their playing schemes), weather(more than 60 years of global weather analysis are used to predict the risk of future extreme events), logistics (smart tucks and smart species, agriculture (monitoring weather and soil conditions for optimum point of harvesting).

Consequently, due to the evolving consumer demands, and the ever growing digitization, the world is digitally transforming which means the new technologies are needed to be used and driven significant business improvement. So, such as why (AI) tool will be our future main predictive tool to help businesses to predict when, how and why their potential customer behavioral will change. Big data is one of the our channels through digital transformation is made, together with cloud, mobile and networks. The challenges for digital transforming and therefore using A I big data gathering tool as main technology are: digital proficiency, legacy systems, security and jobs becoming absolute.

In the future, big data can use data from text to picture , sounds, movies, music satellite coordinates or any other type of input or output data that type of input or output data that came from different influential aspect. It is cloud solutions, bring big data will be for predict insight driven by business strategy, new product strategies and new consumer relationship, predictive consumer behavioral strategy. Using the right data in the right business decision will mean smart decisions, new opportunities and utimately a big competitive advantage. Hence (AI) big data gathering tool is different is that (AI) can be one depth in-memory database function, it can make real-time data analytics that provide meaningful information in short time, it is also the visualization tool , such as SAP Lumira, allow this exploration and understanding of the data, and ultimately supports the decision making process. All above these features, which will be human's data gathering effort who won't exceed (AI) big data gathering effort. Hence, future (AI)big data gathering will be the best choice to assist businesses to predict consumer behaviors successfully.

Reference

Adrian, P. (2012). Introduction to marketing theory & practice, 3 rd edition, London: Oxford press.

Ajzen, I (1991). The theory of planned behavior. Organizational behavior and human decision processes, 50(2), 179-211. doi: 10.1016/0749.5978 (91) 90020-7.

Alba, Joseph W. and J. Wesley Hutchinson (1987). " Dimensions Of Consumer Expertise", Journal of consumer research, 13 March, 411-454.

Bailey, L., Mokhtarian, P.L. Little, A. (2008). The broader Connection Between Public Transportation, Energy Conservation And Greenhouse Gas Reduction, Report Prepared As Part Of TCRP Project J-11/Tasks Transit Cooperative Research Program, Transportation Research Board Submitted To American Public Transportation Association in http://www.apta.com/research/into/online/land_use.cfmi, accessed 17 April 2008.

Baucer, R,"Consumer Bhavior As Risk Taking , In Risk Taking And Information handling In Consumer Behavior", D. Coxceds Harvard University Press, Cambridge, Mass 1976.

Biederman, P. (2008). Travel and tourism, Pearson Prentice Hall, New Jersey.

Bogers, R. P., Brug, J. Van Assema, P., & Dagnetie, P.C. (2004) , Explaining fruit and vegetable consumption: The theory of planned behavior and misconception of personal intake level. Appetite, 42,157-166.

Bolton, Ruth N. (1998), " A Dynamic Model Of The Duration Of The Customer's Relationship With A Continuous Service Provider: The Role Of Satisfaction", Marketing Science, 17 (1), 45-65.

B.Shiv and A. Fedorikhin, " Heart And Min In Conflict: The Interplay Of affect And Cognition In Consumer Decision Making", J. Consumer Res., vol. 26, pp. 278-292, Dec. 1999.

Brown, K.W., Ryan, R.M. Reswell , J.D. (2007). Mindfulness: Theoretical Foundatins And Evidence For Its Salutary Effects. Psychological Inquiry, 18, 211-237.

Burke, R.R. : Behavioral effects of digital signage, J. Advertising Res. 49(2), 180-185 (2009).

Cant, M., Brink , A. & Brijall, S., Consumer behavior, Cape Town, South Africa: Juta, 2006.

Conner, M. & Abraham, C. (2001). Conscientiousness and the theory of planned behavior: Toward a more complete model of the antecedents of intention and behavior. Social psychology bulletin, 27, 1547-1561.

Cooper C. Mallon, K, Leadbetter S, Pollack L, Peipins (2005) , cancer internet search activity on a major search engine, United States 2001 to 2003, J Med Internet Res. 7(3): e36.

Cope, R. R. Cope and H. Davis (2008). Disney's virtual Queues: A strategic opportunity to co-brand services ? Journal of Business & economics research, vol. 6 no10, 13-20.

Cornelia, B.F. (1999) Rural development news, the North Central Regional Center For Rural Development vol. no 24 , IOWA.

Couper, M.P. J. Blair and T. Triplet (1999). A Comparison Of Mail And E-mail For a Survey Of Employees In USA Statistical Agencies. Journal Of Official Statistics, 15, 39-56.

David J. Nowak & Gordon M. Melsler (2016) " Air quality effects of urban trees and parks." National recreation and park association, USA.

Data monitor (2008). The proctor and gamble company. Retrieved Nov. 15 2009 from http://www.datamonitor.com/

De Hollander, A. E. M., J.M. Melse, Elebret & P. G.N. Kramers (1999), " An Aggregate public health indicator to represent the impact of multiple environmental exposures" Epidemiology: 606-617.

De Visser, R.O., & McDonnell, E.J. (2013). " Man points": Masculine capital and young men's health. Health psychology, 32(1), 5-14. doi:10. 1037/a0029045.

Dunn, J & A Neumsister (2002). Knowledge management in the Information age. E. business review, Fall , 37-45. Jounral of service, spring 2011, vol. 4, no1, De Grovte (2009).

Dyer, D., F. Dalzell & R. Olegario (2004). Rising tide. Lessons learned from 165 years of brand building at Procter and Gamble. Boston, MA: Havard Business School Press.

Eysenbach G (2006) Infodemiology: Tracking flu- related searches on the web for syndromic surveillance. American Medical Informatics Associaion Annual Symposium Proceedings , Curran Associates, Red Hook, NY, pp. 244-248.

Ettredge M, Gerdes, J. Karuga , G (2005) Using web- based search data to predict macro-economic statistics. Commun ACM 48: 87-92.

Felce, D. and Perry, J. (1995). Quality of life: A contribution to its definition and measurement, vol. 16, no.1 pp: 51-74.

Feldman, Jack M. And John G. Lynch Jr. (1988), "Self-Generated Validity And Other Effects Of Measurement On Belife, Attitude, Intention And Behavior", Journal of applied psychology, 73(3),421-35.

Fiese, M, Hofmann, W., & Wanke, M (2009). The impulsive consumer. Predicting consumer behavior with implicit reaction time measurement. In M. Wanke (ed.) Social psychology of consumer behavior (pp.335-364). New York, NY: Psychology press.

Fitzsimons, Gavan, J. And Vicki G. Morwitz (1996), " The Effect Of Measuring Intent On Brand-Level
Purchase Behavior", Journal of consumer research, 23 (1), 1-11.

Hallerman , D. (2008) video Advertising Online: Spending And Pricing , New York. E-Marketer.

Harriet Griffey. (2010) The art of concentration, enhance focus, Reduce, stress and achieve move. Macmillan publishers ltd,Basinastoke and Oxford, London UK.

Helleman, D. (2008) Video Advertising Online: Spending And Pricing , New York, E-Marketer.

Hensen, C. (2003). Kreuzfahrtourismus.www.christoph- hensen.de/ Facharbeit.pdf.

Huang, H.I. (2012). An empirical analysis of the strategic Management of competitive advantage: a case study of higher technical and vocational education in Taiwan (Doctoral dissertation,
Victoria University).

Jamieson, Linda F. And Frank M. Bass (1989), " Adjusting Stated Intention Measures To Predict Trial Purchase Of New Products: A Comparison Of Models And Methods," Journal of marketing research, 26 (August), 336-45.

Korea Ministry Of Environment. Public Organizations spend 2.2 Trillon Korean Won To Purchase green Products in 2014; Ministry Of Environment: Sejoung, Korea, 2015.

Kremers, S.P. J., De Bruijn, G.J., droomers, M., Van Lenthe, F. J., & Brug, J. (2005). Environmental interventions for selected dietary behaviors in adults. In J. Brug & F. J. Van Lenthe (eds.) , Environmental determinants and interventions for physical activity, nutrition and smoking: A review pp. 282-315. Rotterdam: Erasmus Medical Center.

Lee, D.; Kim, M. ; Lee, J. adoption of green electricity policies: Investigating the role of environmental attitudes via big data-driven search-queries. Energy policy 2016. 90, 187-201.

Lee, Terrence, " Tech in Asia-connecting Asia's startup system " Tech. in Asia- connecting Asia's startup ecosystem, N.p.,4 July 2016.

Los Angeles Country Department Of public Health (2016), Country Health Ranking Model, Retrieved From www.countryhealthrankgings.org/our-approach. USA.

Mayne, Lonnie. " Evolve of die in the age of the consumer". Entrepreneur, N.P. , 16 Apr. 2014. web of Oct. 2016.

McGregor, S.L. T., & Goldsmith, E.B. (1998). Expanding our understanding of quality of life, standard of living and well-being. Journal of family and consumer science, 90(2), 2-6, 22.

McMichael, A.J. M. Mckee, J. Shkolnikov and T. Valkanen (2004), " Morality trends and setbacks, global convergence or divergence?", Lancet 363, 1155-1159.

Melse, J.M. & A.E. M. De Hollander (2001). " Human Health And The Environment", background document for the OECD Environmental Outlook, OECD, Paris.

Moschis, George p. & Roy, L. Moore (1979), " Decision making among the young. A socialization perspective " Journal of consumer research , 6 (September).

Mulligan, M. Banerjee, T & Thomas, N. (2008) ,European Paid Content And Activity Forecast, (2008 to 2013), Jupiter Research.

Peter, J., Ryan, M, M, " An Investigation Of Perceived Risk At The Brand Level, " Journal of marketing research, 13 May 1976, pp. 184-188.

Pieters, R., & Wedel, M. (2007). Goal Control Of Visual Attention To Advertising: The Yarbus Implication. Journal Of Consumer Research, 34, 224-233 (August).

Parasuaman, and Leonard L. Berry (1985), " Problems And Strategies In Sevices Marketing", Journal of marketing, 49 (Spring), 33-46.

Priesnitz, W. (2007) Counting Our Food Miles. Natural Life, 1 July.

R.C. Oliver, " When is consumer loyalty?" J.Marketing vol. 63, pp.33-44.1999.

Reggiani, A . (ed). 1998, accessibility, trade and locational behavior, Ashgate publishing ltd, England.

Rushe, D. (2013) " The 10 best paid CEO in America". The Guardian , 22 Oct, (online). Available at:
http://www.theguardian.com/business/2013/Oct22/best-paid-chief-executives-america (Accessed: 3 May 2014).

Spiekermann and Wegener (2007), update of selected potential accessibility indicators. Final report, urban and regional research (S&W), RRG spatial planning and geoinformation. ESPON. Available online
at http:// <www.espon.eu/mmp/online/website/ contentprojects/947/ 1297/file_2724/espon_accessibility_update-2006-fr_070207.pdf>, accessed on 1 July 2009.

Starbucks (2014) Our company available at http:// www. starbucks.com/about- us/company-information (accessed: 3 May 2014).

Shostack, G. Lynn (1984), " Designing Services That Deliver", Harvard Business Review, 62 (January-February), 133-9.

Shostack, G. Lynn (1985), " Planning The Service Encounter ,in the service encounter" , John A. Czepiel, Michael R. Solomon, and Carol F. Suprenant, eds. New York: Lexington Books, 243-54.

Shostack, G. Lynn (1987), " Service Positioning Through, Structural Change", Journal of marketing, 51 (Janurary), 34-43.

Soloman, Michael R. (1985), "Packaging The Service Provider", Service Industries Journal , 5(1), 64-71.

Stevens, C.W. (1980), "K-MartStores Try New Look To Invite More Spending" The Wall Street Journal, Nov. 26, 29-35.

Sullivan, Nicholas P(2007). You can hear me now: How Micro loans and cell phones are connecting the world, San Francisco, CA: John Wilsey & Sans, 2007.

T. Ambler, A. Ioannides, And S. Rose, " Brand s On The Brain : Neuroimages Of Advertising ", Business Strategy rev., vol. 11, 3. pp. 17-30. 2000.

Westbrook, Robert A. (1980), " Intrapersonal affective influences on consumer satisfaction with products, " Journal of consumer research , 7 (June) 49-54.

Wiig, k.(1993). Knowledge management foundations: Thinking About thinking. How people and organizations create, represent and use knowledge vol.1 , of knowledge management series schema press: Arlington, TX.

World Health Organization (2003). Diet, nutrition and the prevention of Chronic diseases report of a joint WHO/FAO. expert consultation. Geneva: World Health Organization.

Wysocki, B. (1979), " Sight, Smell, Sound: They're all arms in retailer's arsenal" The Wall Street Journal, Nov. 17, 1979. 1-35.

Yale Center For Environmental Law And Policy (2006). Environmental Performance Index. Data available on-line at http://epi.yale.edu